FOUR PAWS AND A TALE

as told by the dog

MARY BARNES ANDERSON

ISBN: 979-8-89316-065-9 (paperback)
ISBN: 979-8-89316-067-3 (hardcover)
ISBN: 979-8-89316-066-6 (ebook)

Library of Congress Number 2024906944

Dedication

To the owners of these canine stars in our lives

CONTENTS

"Can you tell me what life is like for you?"

Contents

ALL ABOUT ME

Homebody, rover,
entertainer, companion,
teacher, hunter,
confidant, friend.
More ways, more ways.

Content, loyal,
brave, intelligent,
gentle, tough,
faithful, protective.

Day or night,
visible, invisible,
unspoken, tells all.

My home, your home,
in gratitude, more ways.

Love's contract complete.

Whispers from Across the Bridge

Here we come, ready or not,
some slow, some wander,
some dance, some stomp.

The bridge path
has surprises.
Smooth or rugged,
We choose.
Welcome.

Perfection abounds,
no resistance.
Run, play, sleep.
Eyes closed,
it's all there.

The winds carry,
love memories float,
the sun warms,
hearts remember.
The rain refreshes,
no tears.

Tails wag, waving joy.
Hearts know your presence.
With patience and love,
we wait for you.
Always faithful,
our motto.

INTRODUCTION

Many dogs have entered my life. Each of them has a personality and story. **FOUR PAWS AND A TALE as told by the dog,** was written to reveal their lives and bring the reader joy.

I have gathered these narratives from many areas during my RV travels in the USA and from owners who adopted dogs from other countries.

The selection of dogs was either rescued, abandoned, giveaways, bred for specific purposes, or survivors. Like all of us, they have their own story.

Each vignette represents a snapshot of the time when it was written. The question, *"Can you tell me what life is like for you?"* summarizes how their lives began and how they got their names and forever homes. Tales of their adventures with outcomes in daily living add humor. Some stories reveal the lives of dogs that have created memories, such as *"Whispers from Across the Bridge."*

The dogs entered families, some with no expectations and others to be saved or serve as companions. **As told by the dog**, Mom, Dad, relatives, and friends are the ways I relay their communications. Some have asked if I am a *"dog whisperer?"* As for me, I merely listen to them.

The dogs have contributed to a way of life by describing their mannerisms, behaviors, conflicts, and resolutions. It has amazed me how remarkable these stars have enhanced the lives of their owners.

As you read each story, I aim to embody your spirit as you join in the fun and laughter, love and faithfulness, joys and sorrows these dogs have provided by being someone's best friend. Their passion and gratitude have comforted many a lonely heart.

As the author, I gave individualized attention to capture every dog's personality. Dogs are gifts, sometimes apparent and sometimes hidden. Famous for unconditional love, no matter where, why, or how your life unfolds, they are "man's best friend." We can also learn from their instincts. It's no wonder, *dog spelled backward, is God.*

Each dog owner can relate to the magnificence of these canines. Dogs are unique. After reading **FOUR PAWS AND A TALE**, you may want a companion if you are not already a dog owner.

By the way, dogs like to have dog friends, too.

Can you find yourself in these love stories **as told by the dog?**

*"Can you tell me
what life is like for you?"*

Randy

Norman

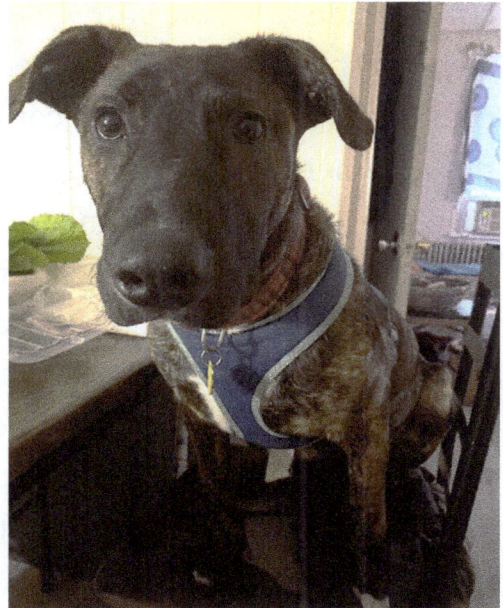

I got lucky. A lady wanted to foster a senior dog, but after seeing my puppy picture, she claimed me and named me *Norman.* When she held me in her arms on our meeting day, I knew we were meant to be together. My forearms hugged her in return.

Living in the inner city of Chicago, I wondered how my new mom would control me in busy residential areas and street traffic. Being a Pit Bull/Great Dane mix, I weighed seventy pounds at six months and was still growing. Since I ran around in circles to burn off energy, my neighbors gave me the nickname *Stormin' Norman.*

One of my routine walks was to a Chinese section of the city where Mom patronized a store with Asian food. The store owner liked me and invited me into his establishment. With a heavy accent, I received another nickname: *Pit Bull Almost.* I didn't receive any snacks at the store, but his attention made me stand up straight and be on my best behavior.

My conduct differed at home, where I could let my hair down. Being observant of what Mom was up to, I wanted to participate in her daily activities. Pushing a chair beside the table sitting near her while she had her morning coffee prompted me to grab whatever she needed to put into her wake-up beverage. Outcomes could have been better, but coffee spilled. I was only trying to be helpful. She replaced her cup with a capped water bottle to solve that temptation.

When Mom did the laundry, I was right there to assist. It became an obsession of mine to remove the clothes out of the basket when the laundry was done and take them to my bed. That displeased her, and I got scolded, which developed into a syndrome: hiccups.

Chores were left to Mom, but I continued to insist on helping.

Boredom around the house caused me to have other outlets. Hide-and-seek was a fun game. Hiding Mom's hairbrush in the towels I took out of the laundry basket made me smile as I watched her frantically look for the brush to pretty up her hair.

One of Mom's proud possessions is her purse. *What's in that pocketbook that's so important?* I discovered a wallet, keys, lipstick, tissues, pencil, and paper and lined up everything I found in a row. Proud of the display, she scolded me, and hiccups started again, a sure sign of remorse. Unfortunately, that didn't stop me from investigating her handbag in the future. After all, she might be playing hide-and-seek on me to find a hidden cookie this time.

Another excellent opportunity for me was to fetch items to line up when Mom closed the bathroom door to shower. Surprise! Not only did I bring her a bath towel, but waiting for her outside the door were cleaning supplies, utensils, and napkins. I mastered arranging my findings in a perfect lineup and was proud.

Potato chips are the only snack that tempts me beyond my control. Mom stores the bag on top of the refrigerator, but being resourceful, I push a chair next to the kitchen counter. *Can you picture what's next?* No problem reaching my favorite snack.

Being an intelligent, innovative dog, I've gotten into trouble with one thing after another. I found it easy to open the refrigerator door to reach my target: the soy sauce and rice Mom brought home from the Asian market.

My mom was always patient with me, but frustration built up within her. I started getting sprayed with a water gun as she said, "NO." The water spray was not my favorite, and I tried to dodge the attack. That led to her using the words, "Spray you." Knowing what that meant, sometimes that discipline worked, and sometimes it didn't.

All my fun things to do were turning into a nightmare for Mom to handle. Her only recourse was to take me to dog training school. Mom and I put on our thinking caps on how to finance my education. The idea of sharing her homemade dog cookies turned into a potential solution. We went into business together. "*Norman's Nuggets*" became a hit at the local farmer's market. I was her sales assistant and the "official cookie taster," which validated the variety of delicious treats. The business was booming. She made enough money to pay for tuition, anticipating being transformed to succeed at home and in my inner-city surroundings. Now, to find the right teacher.

There's a special friend I'd like you to meet. In my small fenced-in backyard, climbing onto the picnic table has become a sign for Sam to visit. Sam is a bird, and we befriended each other. When he landed on my back, his light claws tiptoed across my body, proving his gentleness. Sam never pokes me. I may be a giant, but he knows I have a soft side.

Giving my paw to others in a charming manner, I learned social skills from Mom when I was a puppy. *Will my "puppy-like" habits ever be forgotten?*

As a young whipper-snapper, I needed a step stool to climb into bed. Sleeping in my mom's bed became only big enough for me. Since I'm a big boy, Mom has resorted to sleeping in the recliner.

She's the greatest in the whole world. Her patience and unconditional love have motivated me to become a perfect gentleman. Thanks. I continue to wonder, *Will I still need to go to school?*

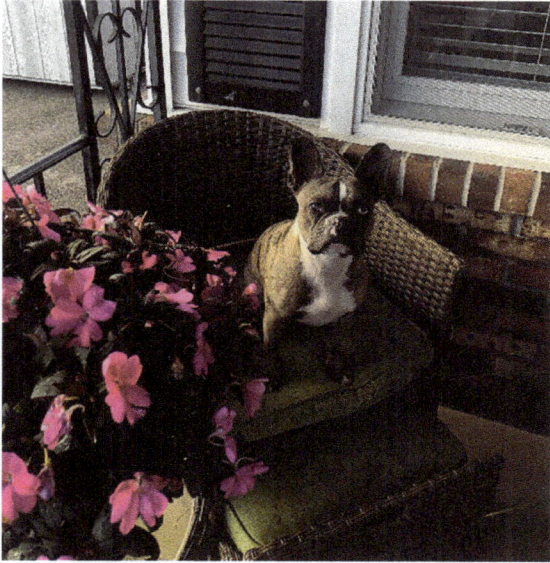

Andee

As a Boston Terrier/French Bulldog, I'm identified as a Merle Blue Frenchton. After an Internet search, a couple drove several hundred miles to see me. Only eight weeks old, I wasn't sure what to expect. With much enthusiasm, it was love at first sight. Even though it was a long ride to my new home, sleeping most of the way made it seem like a blink of an eye.

I was named after their favorite Aunt Dee. Being a male dog, I knew I was not expected to follow in the footsteps of a female relative, especially after Mom and Dad named me Andee.

As a young puppy, I quickly became socialized. After graduating from basic training, which included the commands necessary to be well-behaved, I qualified for intermediate classes. It was mostly the same stuff but more demanding. My diplomas are proudly displayed on the living room wall. *Do I always obey commands, even though I know them by heart?* My answer is yes and no, only when I want to. I'm not stubborn, just energetic.

I continue to go to a six-hour daycare once a week, and being with friends is a highlight. My energy carries over in many ways. One of my favorite activities is playing at the off-leash dog park. As a pack leader, I encourage Maddie, Scout, and Randy to chase me. We all run fast and efficiently to dodge obstacles.

Around the house, I tempt Mom to chase me. One of the stop-off points is on top of the dining room table. I'm still learning the word "No."

Mom likes to hide my prize possessions, and being a detective, I stare in front of a secure cabinet until she returns them to me. The face on my favorite blue puppy toy can distract me sometimes but doesn't calm my energy.

When Dad sits in the recliner, and I hop on his lap, that's a sure sign it's time to relax and steal a few winks.

Outings can include trips to Pennsylvania, Tennessee, and Georgia, which have taught me to be on my best behavior, especially at restaurants.

There are entertainment parties every St. Patrick's Day. When the festive music starts, my dad is invited to do the Irish Jig. I've learned the steps to join in, even though I'm still perfecting my dance.

Inflated balloons are another party favorite. I can hold the tip in my mouth without bursting it while running throughout the house. Resting on top of the balloon tickles my belly. Everyone laughs. I'm the life of the party. I can do all these things without drinking green beer. I wear my green hat and beads around my neck like everyone else. I'd love it if St. Patrick's Day came more than once a year.

My favorite meals include chicken, but I don't beg. Whatever Mom gives me is always a great meal. I weigh 20 lbs. and won't get much heavier.

Days are full after my energy runs down. Sleep comes quickly as I Velcro next to my parents under the covers. I'm a happy dog.

Sarg

I was rescued at eight weeks old. Before that, I was too young to remember my first family. Being a handsome pit bull puppy, I was warmly welcomed into a second home. With loving attention, I quickly learned to sit and shake hands, which made my new mom proud of me.

As I grew older, I became accustomed to being a stay-at-home dog. Walks and outside activities were less important to me. However, my curiosity spiked when Mom returned from an outing. The scent on her clothes was a clue that other dogs were in her presence. The laundry basket needed further investigation to confirm my suspicions.

I thought I knew everything about Mom, but one day, she left home and didn't return for a long time. Days turned into weeks and then into months. Even though I had lots of care from relatives, I pined for her with an aching heart. It felt like forever, and I wondered if she'd ever be with me again.

Leaped with joy, happy days came. Mom returned after a long separation. This time, there was an unusual scent that intrigued me. It wasn't a dog. It wasn't food.

It wasn't from shopping. It wasn't a smell I ever encountered before. She was hospitalized, and those new scents alerted me that something was wrong.

Mom suffered an injury and needed my love and attention, so I gave it to her. I cuddled up closely, laid my head on her chest, and listened to the soft rhythm of her heartbeat. It was music to my ears. We were both comforted. Recovery was slow, but I was patient.

When playtime once again resumed, I knew Mom was OK. Overpowering squeaky stuffed animals gave me pleasure. Once they didn't speak anymore, my interest in them faded.

I love to sink my teeth into plastic bottles. For some reason, the crunching noise doesn't stop, and I can't control the crackles. Squeaky toys, I can conquer, but the plastic bottle sound remains a challenge. For some reason, they continue to talk back to me. I have the virtue of perseverance.

The fenced-in backyard has a doghouse, which I never occupy and remains empty. I prefer my residence to be indoors; that suits me better.

Wiggling my toes in the water is acceptable. I shy away from full-body dunks in the outside pool. Others can splash and have fun; I prefer watching them from afar.

I often wondered how I got the name *Sarg. Is it because Mom thinks I rule the house like a military sergeant?* She usually responds with, "Yes, Sir." I look distinguished enough to demand attention, but I obey when the commander-in-chief (Mom) gives an order. One of her demands is getting my nails clipped. I need to be presentable if I want to shake hands at parties.

Another rule at parties is that everyone, including me, must wear a hat. From reindeer horns at Christmas, Halloween hats for scary times, and clown hats for summer fun, no matter the occasion: hats, hats. That's not my idea of fun, but I recognize pizza boxes, which translates into party time. I prefer my slices cut into small pieces and fed to me with a fork. I tried more giant slices, but that didn't work. Too hard to handle, and then I must lick my paws if I want to shake hands again.

Another snack I enjoy is toast, only if it has butter on it. Having a good appetite satisfies me.

One of my favorite resting spots is guarding the house before the bay window. When the doorbell rings and someone is at the entry, I harmonize with barking. Day or night, I protect my best friend and others who took care of me. They know how much I love them. Their return love is what makes me a happy dog.

Let's go for a walk.

Storm

Somewhere in Iowa, the home of miles and miles of cornfields, a breeder of Yellow Labs had a "puppy mill." Even though many of us looked alike, *was it my personality and disposition that stood out to adopt me on sight? Or was it because I was a male who would grow up big and powerful?* I had no idea what was in store for me.

Relocating to a farm in New Jersey, the familiarity of corn fields made me feel at home with the added benefit of no kennels. The farm had a massive amount of land. Running to my heart's content, I darted in and out of the tall stalks. My leaping skills allowed me to be a masterful Frisbee catcher.

Soon, I discovered I'd have two lifestyles, one on land and one at sea. My dad was a commercial fisherman and a perpetually alert captain. Thus, I was given the name *Storm*, but I later discovered my full name was *Storm Warning*.

His fishing vessel was big enough for several crew members, and for me to be included, it hindered no one. I had a sleeping bunk I could call all my own.

Seeing fish jump in the water excited me, so I got into trouble several times by joining them. The dolphins and I swam together in unison. Swimming came naturally, but getting back into the boat was a challenge. Dad had to lasso me with a rope, and with added help, I was pulled back on board.

After several fun times swimming overboard, the captain's orders were, "No more swimming off a fishing vessel." Dad protected the dolphins. My alternative was to stand on the boat's bow, howling and crying, which made me more eager. The next best thing was to dance on deck around the flopping fish that would go to market.

Sometimes, I got in the way of a large catch, and Dad would call out, "Storm, chill out. Go to the wheelhouse." I was grounded, and missing all the action made me sad.

Meals at sea had no routine, and I ate when hungry. A 40 lb. bag of dry dog food was cut open with a fishing knife. No special eating bowls were necessary. Occasionally, I made plentiful sushi recipes, and having a bucket of fresh water was great.

After a strenuous balancing act from the rough seas, the boat was brought in to unload the catch. Everyone looked forward to devouring pizza. *Like father, like son, I enjoyed a beer with my slice.* When the gang played Led Zeppelin[1] songs, it brought out the best in me, and I'd sing along.

Commercial fishing was exhausting. Back to the farm for bed rest. There were many trips back and forth from fishing to home and back to the docks. The trips were about sixty miles each way. Dad frequently stopped for take-out burgers. Since he had to clean up the truck from the pickles I discarded, he got the message and ordered two burgers for me with no pickles, mustard, or ketchup. I wasn't crazy about fries, either.

Our fishing lifestyle lasted for years. If excluded from a trip, I boarded with my dad's girlfriend. Being left behind, I'd let my opinion be known by non-stop barking. One day, a neighbor came to visit me. Thinking it was a pleasant gesture, he took me for a long ride, but it didn't end up friendly. I was dropped off in the woods far from home.

---

[1] Led Zeppelin is an English rock band formed in London in 1968.

Several days went by. Scratched by dry branches and bushes and with nothing to eat, I wondered if Dad would ever find me. Everything looked the same in the Pine Barrens.[2]

My yearning for Dad was relieved. Being missing, he told me the whole story of how desperate and panic-stricken he was. My dad contacted a California Psychic[3] with the request to locate a lost dog. She found me. The outcome intrigued a local newspaper[4] which wanted to print an article. Our reunion was one of the most incredible days of my life.

No fishing? OK, I'm happy to go camping. One day at a campsite, I fell off the tailgate of a pickup truck and landed on my butt. *What happened to my tail?* I thanked my lucky stars that the truck was parked near our tent. I cried, and Dad put his healing hands over my crooked tail. He relieved my pain, but no one will ever be allowed to mess with my tail, even to pull it playfully. My tail remained crooked for life.

Life had its ups and downs. Aging didn't fit into fishing anymore. My uncle gave me a home with his Yellow Lab, Barney, a young "whipper snapper." Barney would nudge me to go swimming, and we often got into trouble at a nearby pond at a private golf course. We ignored the posted "No Swimming" sign.

Barney kept me spry, but his energy became too much for me as a senior. I'd often daydream about how we swam together and jointly carried branches in our mouths.

---

[2] The New Jersey Pine Barrens, also known as the Pinelands or simply the Pines, is the most prominent remaining example of the Atlantic coastal pine barrens ecosystem, stretching across more than seven counties of New Jersey. Wikipedia

[3] California Psychic: No permission was granted to identify.

[4] Newspaper out of business. No longer available

Even though I missed my dad, I liked living with my uncle and Barney. Eventually, sleep became a priority, which is precisely what I did. I slept and slept. I had a life like none other. I fished, worked, partied, and had a best friend. At the age of 15, I retired. Wow! What a life!

Sammy
(New York)

My life had many ups and downs. I can't remember all the places I lived before. I recalled being uprooted several times, resulting in abandonment and anxiety. *I don't know why no one wanted to give me a forever home*, which puzzled me. Having a reputation as a reject from other families, I doubted if anyone would ever adopt me.

Then, a twelve-year-old boy came to the pound seeking a dog for a companion. Indeed, I wasn't selected due to my history but was adopted because the price was right. In other words, I was cheap. Because he accepted me for who I am, I knew there was potential for us to become best buddies if given the chance.

My name, *Sammy*, remained the same, and my ingrained behaviors also remained the same. There was yet to be any trustworthiness established. First, we had to discover each other.

Initially, I tried running away, but the boy caught up, bringing me back home. Questioning my motives to abscond, I realized he liked me. Accepting the offer to sleep in his room was a welcomed sign.

The attempts I made to run away turned into running alongside my friend. When he rode his bicycle, I kept up with him. Laughter, because of my waddling gate, was described as goofy. Our bonding gave me a sense of security; happiness was slowly entering my life.

Past hunger issues created a habit of ripping into the garbage as I knocked down trash cans. Doing my best to overcome this character defect, I often got two meal servings, one from my buddy and one from his dad when he came home from work. *Why? Because I pretended that I hadn't eaten any food yet.* Gaining weight was the tell-tale sign of overeating. To stay fit, I was placed on a diet. My favorite bacon snack had a reduced portion, but licking the dinner plates substituted for dessert.

If I got tired lying around the house and wanted to go outside, I perfected a skill to open the glass sliding door. It took much practice, but I finally got the hang of it. My reward was rolling in the grass or a walk along the banks of a pond. By the way, I skirted around mud puddles. With a sense of available freedom, I didn't need to run away anymore.

Unexpectedly, old memories surfaced. Traveling in a car from the New York Catskill Mountains to New Jersey made me car sick, and visiting a strange place, the anxiety of losing my forever home, frightened me. Home away from home lasted several days. I wasn't invited when my buddy and other family members left me alone to dine at a restaurant. Being scared turned into panic. As I leaped to look out of every window available and watched them drive away, I dismantled the Venetian blinds and cleared my view. Hyperactivity took over me like a bulldozer, and many things got broken.

Needless to say, when everyone returned, I was labeled as a *bad dog.* A new plan was implemented to solve my anxiety and frustration. The next time everyone left me alone, I was confined to a crate with a large plastic tray and a comfortable blanket to cuddle. I destroyed that, too, by chewing the plastic tray into pieces, tearing the veil to shreds, and, being uncontrollably upset, I peed and made a mess out of everything. My howling was loud enough to alarm unresponsive, curious neighbors. My cries: *SAVE ME!* All I wanted was the comfort of my buddy.

When life came back to normal for me, back home in New York, my buddy and I had a long talk as we gazed into each other's eyes. Secretly, he told me he had lost someone very close and dear to him, and our companionship was vital. The fear of losing my buddy, who had become my best friend, would be like losing my lifeline. We understood each other, which cemented our bond more than ever. The acceptance of this young boy gave me a chance and taught me what love is all about. There's no doubt that _this is_ my forever home.

Briar-of-the-Pines

Coming from a breeder of Chocolate Labradors, I was adopted by a man who wanted an exceptional male dog as a companion. Ready to please, my innate confidence displayed sturdiness, intelligence, and friendliness, summing up that I was the perfect choice.

My new home, located near an expansive, thick, overgrown Pine Barrens with a refreshing aroma, became the perfect place to experience trampling through the briars. Even though they were prickly on my skin, I ignored the feeling. After frequent hiking with Dad, I understood why I was named *Briar-of-the-Pines.*

Even though wooded areas were challenging, conversations about how a dog's life can be like those of people, I started daily homeschooling on how to deal with obstacles.

When I was nine months old, my skills included climbing a ladder, walking on a single beam, and jumping through a hoop. Zipping down sliding board ramps was fast and furious. Perfecting my balance on a seesaw took significant concentration so I would not fall off with a jolt. Hearing *"Good boy"* was the only reward.

Exercise was important for both Dad and me. While riding his bicycle, I ran beside him, no matter the speed. When Dad got tired, it was OK to stop.

These activities were fun, but I yearned for more. Behavior was important to Dad. The next challenge was accompanying him as a respected gentleman wherever he went. Before long, I mastered the assignments to be a "Canine Good Citizen."[1] Proudly, I carried my blue ribbon in my mouth.

Imitating him started to become a priority. Paying full attention to detail, I noticed how he picked up the mail every day at the end of the driveway. That was a chore I could handle. Hearing the mail truck on the road stop and start, I waited patiently before it got to my driveway, and then I'd bark to inform the postal driver it was my turn to be of service. Bringing the mail to Dad, including carrying boxes, gave me added purpose. Sometimes, the different delivery personnel thought I only wanted conversation. My impatience surfaced then, and my hair would stand up on my back. Doing my job was more important than chit-chat, and training the carrier to do their job by giving "me" the mail fulfilled my assignment.

---

[1] American Kennel Club designations for performing ten tasks. See the Reference page.

Store advertising flyers displayed limited quantities of certain items, which kept my basket manageable. I loved shopping with Dad. Customers stopped to talk to me, and being a good citizen, I was patient and listened to their monologue. Often, I heard comments, "I never saw a dog like this before." Dad was proud of me.

Exercise, chores, and shopping became a routine.

The next training wasn't homeschooling. It was serious business. Wounded animals, mostly deer, needed to be found and recovered. As I was diligent from hiking in the woods, my newfound skills included being a Certified Blood Tracker.[2]

Counting on my predicted behavior and escorting Dad to medical visits, I listened with full attention when the doctor spoke. Even though it was premature, I felt prompted to assume additional chores, like bringing in groceries, opening and closing the refrigerator, and retrieving the phone. Having a solid muscular back to lean on, Dad taught me how to help him get up from the floor if he needed assistance from an unexpected fall.

Being intuitive, I wondered if this is why Dad wanted to teach me all these life obstacles in our early talks when I was a young pup. By the way, even though I can

_____

[2]   The role of a blood tracker is to save lives, not destroy. See the Reference page.

do many things, I don't carry Dad's fishing pole because he finds joy in doing that for himself.

The cultivated lifestyle I developed has been rewarding and continues every day. However, practicing the golden rule, confirmed by the pheromones of others, is instinctive; no training is necessary.

There's teamwork at mealtime. As Dad fills my bowl with kibbles and a sardine, I close the cupboard door behind him.

I won't tell you about the trouble I get myself into on off-duty hours. I don't want Dad to know about it. Keeping it to myself adds to a secret side of me.

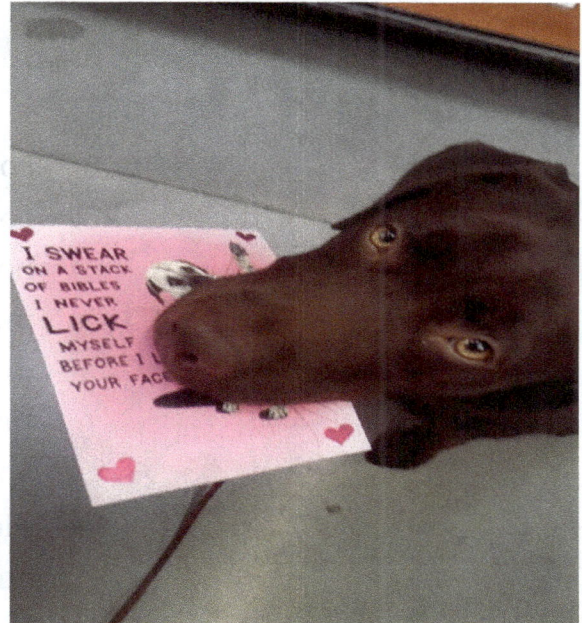

Being told I have become an exceptional dog accepting compliments, I continue to remain humble. *Why? For me, life's essential lessons have been giving and receiving joy.* Dad and I have bonded with a deep love. Thanks for being my role model.

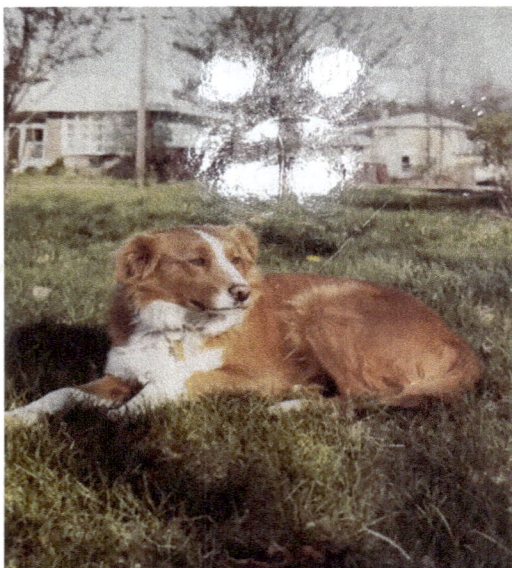

Chipper

A seven-year-old boy wanted a daily companion to play with and love. He had to convince his parents that having a dog was the best thing in the world. Being a mixed-breed male dog, I was happy to be part of his dream. I discovered crunchy potato chips were this boy's favorite snack. We'd sit together on the ground and share this salty treat. What a great guy! It didn't take long for us to become best friends, and calling out *Chipper* meant two things: snack time, and it became my name.

My new family made me a doghouse. I could never decide where I wanted it in the backyard. It was boring having my house in the exact location. Sometimes, it was too sunny, too windy, or too muddy. I dragged my hut around the yard, always wanting a permanent spot. Finally, I concluded I'd rather sleep indoors with everyone else.

Going to Grandma's for an Italian spaghetti dinner became a Sunday tradition. She never saw me eat my share of her home-cooked meal. Secretly, I would dig a hole and bury it. My family never found out where I hid the spaghetti or if I ate it later.

One day, not a spaghetti dinner day, we all hopped in a car, about a five-mile drive, and went to a restaurant that cooked barbeque chicken on an outside grill. The smell was something I'll never forget. Inhaling the aroma made my mouth water. *Sorry, Grandma, chicken took priority over spaghetti.*

I gave myself lots of freedom by wandering off for a few days at a time. I liked keeping secrets. My whereabouts puzzled my family. They'd send out a search and rescue team to look for me, and since I always returned, they accepted that I was probably playing with other dogs. They sighed with relief upon my return, another one of Chipper's outings.

Memories of frequent tantalizing visits and mental notes on how to get the zesty BBQ chicken turned into three-day walking journeys to achieve my goal. I could always tell when I was on the right path because the smell in the airwaves would churn the juices in my belly. The temptations each time were worth the long trips.

My secret was eventually revealed. The restaurant owner "spilled the beans" and told my family I came often for chicken dinner. I wouldn't say I liked the biscuits. The chicken was just fine. After a satisfying meal, home awaited me. I knew how to bang on the door with my paw to reveal that Chipper was back. My buddy was always so excited to see me come home, even though he told me he had been worried when I was gone for days.

After one of my long trips away, it was not an ordinary excursion. I was injured after being hit by a car. I struggled all the way home for help. Bruises and lacerations needed the immediate attention of a vet. It took weeks of love and care before I recovered. My family treated me to BBQ chicken to ease the pain.

On a follow-up visit, I noticed a revealing poster at the vet's office about things to keep away from dogs. There was a picture of a lady's stocking that looked interesting. Shortly after that, I found a hose in the trash and ate it. Not a good idea. When it came time to let nature take its course, I had to have help to remove it. Push and pull. I am embarrassed to highlight this story so you can use your imagination. From then on, I ignored any signs with pictures at the vet's office since there might be a temptation to satisfy my curiosity.

I had lots of fun with the young boy who named me. He faithfully looked forward to seeing me when he got home from school. Summers were everyday fun times together. As he got older, that meant I got older too. My two-to-three-day outings came to an end after sixteen years. I became satisfied with digging holes in the backyard and lying in them. No one ever found the spaghetti hiding places.

I had all the comforts of home and all the freedom a dog could ever want. Over fifty years have passed, and my friend still remembers my tales. These unforgettable memories have been engraved in all the family. I am convinced that I was the best thing in the whole world for my friend. Every time he eats potato chips, it reminds him of me – his *old Chipper.* That's what love and memories are all about.

Lincoln, Mucca, and Harley

I came from a breeder of Great Danes. We're known to be affectionate with children despite our towering size.

Being naïve, I had no idea what adoption would entail, but I was open to it and eager. Nor did I realize I'd be assigned an important job.

Soon after that, I found myself in a forever home and was named *Lincoln*. I became the perfect companion for a young boy. Seeing a strange chair taller than me with slow-moving wheels was occupied by my new buddy. It didn't take long, though, before I grew up and could see him eye-to-eye. His thoughts were my thoughts, and I knew what he wanted or needed. I picked up things that dropped on the floor for him. We watched TV together, and I gave him kisses without demand and knew the sounds of his snores while sleeping. I was his daily buddy. Most importantly, I alerted Mom when he needed special attention.

After about four years, my buddy started going to daycare. Being home alone without him saddened my heart. Mom thought I might want a friend.

So, *Harley* became part of the household. Being related to me from my dad's side, she called me Uncle Lincoln. She was named after a motorcycle. What a relief to know that wasn't my buddy's method of transportation. Those wheels would have been too fast for him.

At times, Harley could be very annoying. She barked a lot and stopped only when she got what she wanted. It could be for snacks, ball playing, or walks. Sometimes, we never knew what was on her mind. If Mom didn't respond right away, her demands were made known by flipping her dish.

When Harley jumped up and put her two front paws on my buddy's wheelchair, it scared me, even though it was to give him kisses. She was often tempted to make food disappear by resting her chin on the edge of the kitchen table. My buddy's outbursts of laughter didn't encourage Harley to stop. As the senior in the house with manners, I wanted to teach her right from wrong by being patient and tolerating those behaviors. Eventually, I accepted that laughter was the best medicine.

HARLEY, barking, as usual, had something to say.

One day, when Mom and I were in the car driving on the freeway, my antenna alerted me when we saw a small dog on the side of the road. I wondered how long she was left there, dirty and hungry. Mom stopped, and my nurturing instinct immediately wanted to bring her home.

This abandoned mixed-breed dog had black and white spots like a baby cow. That's how *Mucca* got her name. (*Mucca means calf in Italian).* I figured she'd grow up but smaller than Uncle Lincoln or me. Mucca was petrified by everything during her first month living with us. After overcoming her fears, *I wondered if she could be attempting to imitate being a Great Dane.* Instantly, I canceled that thought.

There was no way she was one of us. She's too small. We are big, powerful, and intelligent.

Mucca was always getting into trouble: chewing up shoes, stealing food within her reach, and hiding and shredding things into pieces. My Uncle and I called her "an aggressive little brat." Sheepishly, it reminded me of my youthful days when I took food from the kitchen table.

A pack leader, she is not but thinks she is. After two years, Mucca still doesn't know her rank in the house. Uncle Lincoln is alpha. She has grown to weigh 50 lbs, but as Great Danes, we each weigh over 100 lbs more than her. If we wanted to, we could step on her and hold her down, but we are kind.

We love beach outings. As for me, I like jumping into the waves, Mucca likes splashing in the shallow water, and Uncle Lincoln thinks his role is being a lifeguard. He wants to supervise to get a tan.

Mucca likes to be with others. As she looks at us with pitiful eyes, we do our best to console her with our company. Mom used to relax on a large sofa. You guessed it. The couch has become a bed for the three of us. We share.

Time has brought us all together as a family. Even Mucca

looks forward to our buddy's return from daycare. Our home has an elevator to get the wheelchair into the house. Wagging our tails, we greet him with kisses, kisses, and more kisses.

Jolene and Tater

Did you tell us that . . .
INTERNATIONAL DOG DAY IS AUGUST 26TH

Kalea

I was born and raised on the Hawaiian Island of Maui, the rainbow capital of the world. At three months old, I was spotted standing atop a car, surveying my surroundings while wandering the streets. The casual lifestyle here with warm open breezes brought frequent vacationers, and they stopped to talk to me.

Without any expectations, a man living nearby offered me a permanent home. Gently, he put a harness on me, and I happily accepted it. I was given the name *Kalea*, the native meaning for a bright and joyful personality.

Having the proverbial courage of a female American Staffordshire Terrier mixed with the unlimited energy of a Jack Russell Terrier, I took to the water immediately like an Olympic athlete. The azure waters were inviting; my affinity for the ocean suited my new dad. Boating and scuba diving captivated his enthusiasm, and I became his perfect companion.

Fitted for a life jacket, adventures at sea evolved into swimming and game playing. I learned to retrieve a float rope, a sport I looked forward to until…

ONE DAY, WITHOUT WARNING, a vast wave tossed me around. *What happened to the calm Pacific Ocean?* Gratefully, the surge didn't consume me, and I continued to swim. A colossal tail rose from the depths of the ocean. I was surprised and startled at the same time. My lifejacket kept me afloat, and my curiosity wanted to get closer to investigate.

Before my eyes, it was hard to imagine how something gigantic could appear from beneath the sea. The sounds this creature made were alluring. *Was it calling me?* Responding with my magnanimous personality, I made friends with a Humpback whale. That memorable experience was embedded in my mind, but gulping the warm salt water wasn't appealing. On a subsequent boat trip, I was satisfied to plunge into the water and retrieve the float rope when the whale remembered me and followed me back to the boat. *Was it curiosity, or did the whale also want to play fetch?*

Sea trips were frequent. On another occasion, while still onboard, the whale spotted the boat and approached. It circled us several times with its unusual vocal sounds.

Being excited, Dad anticipated my relentless tail wagging might throw me overboard. He informed me that the Island Authorities prohibited swimming with the whales. Obeying the command of *NO*, I restrained myself. I pretended there was an invisible fence between me and the deep blue sea.

Curling up my paws, I firmly braced myself to hold on and forfeited joining my new friend. Showtime of splashing and breaching, the whale entertained us both before it swam away. The white waters became calm once again.

As our friendship grew, Mama Whale returned with her baby. Her peals were indeed a trusting sound. As I peered into Dad's eyes, the amazement of how the whale followed us told the whole story of a formed alliance.

Back home on land, I romped with my piglet friend, named *Spam*, but our interaction didn't last long. In the blink of an eye, he grew overnight and weighed much more than my thirty-five pounds, which slowed him down. He was like a fixture, hanging out and observing his surroundings.

However, Spam was not as sluggish as the giant tortoise, Tequila, who was also part of our family.

In addition, Dad invited a dog named *Charlie* to live with us. Charlie's fun was poking Tequila's hard shell to move faster, but I've accepted that the turtle had his own mind. Tequila was content browsing around, looking for veggies anywhere to be found.

My favorite ball needed protection, so it was off-limits to my canine friend. I didn't share my toys with him. We did, however, become swimming partners off the beach, yet I couldn't convince Charlie to join Dad and me on the boat. Charlie remained at home to be a guard dog.

It was always a joy to have my buddy greet me when I returned from a sea trip, but with tired *sea legs,* I was exhausted. He understood that playtime was on hold; sleep was a priority. Charlie was okay with me if I smelled of seaweed or fish.

Dad's spoken words have enhanced our inseparable communication. Sometimes, he conveyed stories about massive land areas where it snowed and used to live. *What was snow? I couldn't visualize anything like that. Where would I swim?* It would be like a fish out of water.

The perfect island weather is my home. Wherever my imagination might take me, land or sea, being with Dad is good enough for me. I thrive on love-feeding love, and the original Hawaiian name of Kalea humbles me. Gratitude tells me life is good.

Double Rainbow on the Hawaiian Island of Maui
Picture compliments of
MauiOutdoors.com
Visit the website for items designed in Maui

Joey

I was the oddball in a litter of Mini-Schnauzers. I ended up in a specialized rescue center designated for my breed. Being born bigger than my siblings and having all white hair, these two strikes against me disqualified me from ever being a "show dog." Even though I was rejected from that category, I still had confidence that I'd be adopted, regardless of no exhibition potential.

A couple visited the kennels and were explicitly searching for my breed. I stood out from others because I looked different. Typically, Schnauzers' coats are black and silver. They pointed at me as I ran through the play-yard, so I knew my charm captured them. Off I went, and I was named *Joey* on the drive home with my new parents.

It didn't take long for my hyperactivity to cause them stress. As seniors, they had difficulty keeping up with my unlimited energy. Doubts crept into their minds, and I wasn't sure if they would keep me. There were return policies.

As I listened in on their conversation, my ears perked up. They decided to enroll me in training classes. It was either learn and perform, or they would boot me out of my new home. The way their voices sounded, there would be no regrets if I was gone.

Classes were demanding, and being a terrier, I was called a *holy terror.* The course had twelve other canines; some were timid, outgoing, distracted, and constantly yapping. Indeed, only an experienced trainer could handle such diversity. I took mental notes. The six challenging weeks seemed to take forever, and graduation day finally arrived. The trainer informed everyone that if their diploma was signed, it meant that the dog passed the curriculum. No signature on the certificate only acknowledged their attendance and no passing grade. Surprisingly, there was only one graduate. *Guess who? It was me*! My parents were proud. Now, I had to live up to their expectations.

Going on walks was one of my favorite things, but I never liked walking with a leash. If Mom had walked a mile, I must have walked two miles because I darted everywhere regardless of my schooling. Being introduced to the off-leash dog park was perfect for me. As a bonus, three times a week. I visited a daycare play yard to provide socialization, whatever that meant.

Yapping at just about everything was my way of communicating. My dad hushed me, but my mom's polite mannerism would say, "Thank you for telling me." *Hooray!* She figured me out, and I'd stop barking. Dad would scratch his head, "What just happened?" Having two masters confused me at times.

Something sad and unexpected happened. My dad had a heart attack and was no longer with us. I *really* had to step up to the plate. My personality dramatically changed from that day, and I became a devoted, loyal companion.

Taking care of Mom and wanting to please her, I became the most obedient dog in the whole wide world. My acceptable behaviors allowed me to tag along with her everywhere she went. At nursing home visits, I was considered an unofficial therapy dog. Going to the office with her on work days, I'd sit patiently in the doorway until I was invited to enter. The training sessions paid off. She was proud of me once again.

On one of our routine walks, Mom lost her house key. After tracing our steps several times, my sniffing abilities failed to find it. She panicked. Being locked out of the house, I came to the rescue by going in and out of my doggie door built into the side wall of our home. Unfortunately, Mom was too big to wiggle through the opening and follow me in, but it gave her an insightful message. A three-year-old boy in the neighborhood was up for the challenge. It was like magic. As I led the way, the boy crawled behind me, and *viola,* the door opened—no need for a locksmith. Afterward, a key was hidden under a flower pot for security.

Mom had two heroes: I was #1, and the young lad was #1. My reward was hugs and kisses. As a thank you, she knitted a cap for the child and labeled it. To: *My hero!* From: *"Guess who?"*

Another unforeseen incident struck! As we routinely walked through the neighborhood, a large yellow lab came out of nowhere and attacked me. I was minding my own business when this stray dog must have thought I was a rabbit. Everything happened so quickly. Mom cried all the way to the animal hospital. My life was over in a flash.

The vet was highly empathetic when he told her my body was gone, but my spirit would find *a new right dog and immediately go to the Humane Society.* Being so traumatized, she didn't accept what the vet told her to do, but he insisted.

Mom was devastated that I was gone, so she prayed. As I looked down from dog heaven, my spirit felt like I was in two places. One place was with her, and the other was at the shelter.

A small dog named Randy was boarded at the kennel for over two months. He looked ragged with long black matted hair and was very shy. I assured this puppy he would soon be adopted, and I would give him the courage by being his sidekick when my mom would come to find him.

Informing Randy that she was a senior with specific likes and dislikes, there would be requirements, and that's why I was sent to school. Hyperactivity was high on the list of *no-noes.* Randy listened to me attentively, and sure enough, when my mom came, they both were attracted to each other. I was proud of my choice for her.

After five years, I left with many good memories. My whispers to Randy from across the bridge made me know that my life had completed a purposeful mission. Mom has continued to remember all my endeavors with love and gratitude. We were perfect for each other.

NOTE: This is Part I. Park II continues with Randy's story.

Part II

Randy

I was born in a desert area of Southern California near Mexico but only lived there briefly. Unknown circumstances changed, and I found myself at a Humane Society. The kennels were overcrowded, and many dogs were transported to various shelters throughout the state. While at my new location for two months, I looked unkempt. My hair grew long and matted. *Would I be welcomed in anyone's home?*

Then, one day, my demeanor perked up when the sentient presence of another dog surrounded me, yet there was no other physical dog. Sensing a message from the unknown, I was assured I'd be adopted soon.

The kennel had regular business hours. For several consecutive days, the same lady came to visit. Our eyes met, leading to her talking to me, petting me, and holding me in her arms. That was the welcoming change I was waiting for.

Listening to her attentively, she told me the story about Joey. After hearing her experience of Joey's traumatic passing, while in prayer and meditation, a small still voice inside her said, *"Your next dog is named Randy."* Goose bumps covered her arms, and chills made her shake. I was *that* Randy.

Good news came from a kennel attendant. I was going to have a new home.

Immediately, a groomer was selected to give me a haircut, just like Joey's style. Being a Lasha-poo, it wasn't a typical cut for my breed, but that's what that lady wanted.

I took heed of Joey's advice. My new mom wanted an excellent walker that didn't constantly pull on the leash like he did. No problem, I was happy to comply. The walks were pleasurable—conversation, humming, or singing filled us joyfully.

It took several months to adjust to my new living arrangements, but only one day to bond with my new mom. My security was knowing where she was at every moment. When she left the house to go on errands, anxiety crept in, and upon her return, my labored breathing confirmed my fears.

Necessary shopping became a challenge for her. The questions were: *when to leave the house, and when not to?* My panic problem was solved when Mom's shopping trips were accomplished in the evenings when the temperature was cool. I waited in the car with no breathing issues.

Another evening activity Mom enjoyed was knitting when her workday was over. My curiosity got me into trouble on several occasions. Yarn parties, while Mom was fast asleep, were so much fun. Proficient at grasping one end of the yarn in my mouth, I ran through the house, wrapping the long strands around the dining room table and in and out the doggie door. After the yarn got too tangled, I'd conk out and go to sleep.

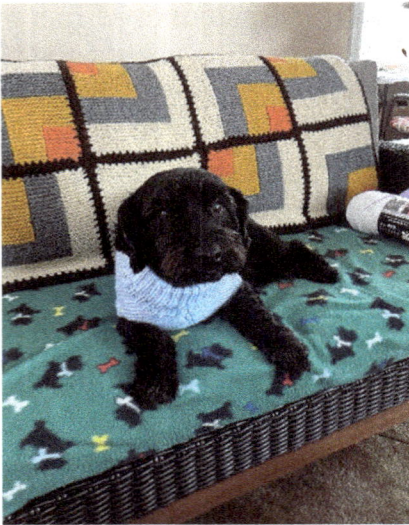

Another solution was needed. Next to my mom's sofa was an old-fashioned bread box to hide the yarn. It had a drop-down door. Watching very closely how to open it, I mastered that task.

Mom and I had a long talk about her knitting hobby. Since my enthusiasm for yarn was evident, she made me a sweater. Wearing it proudly, I discontinued my antics with mile-long threads. My wardrobe slowly increased, and eventually, I had multiple sweaters to pick and choose from.

My sweater comforted me, and I was no longer anxious when Mom went on her errands or grocery shopping. Being home alone to guard the house became my priority.

My lifestyle changed when my uncle came to live with us temporarily. He was a long-range fisherman. Making round trips in an RV became routine. The destination to the port-of-call was the coast of Oregon. Crabbing was not my cup of tea because I had to wear slickers, which didn't fit me well. However, requirements were requirements.

With raging storms and rogue waves at sea, an unexpected tragedy struck. No more fishing vessel; no more uncle. A permanent loss. Mom's sadness turned into depending on me for comfort. I stayed by her side every moment, day and night. We moved from the Coast of the Pacific Ocean to the Coast of the Atlantic, a three-thousand-mile RV trip.

The trip started with a visit to the Redwood forests in Northern California. Riding in an antique steam locomotive train was like going through tunnels of branches with only dots of sunlight peeking through. I never saw tall trees like that before, and when the ride was over, I could pee on one of these giants that reached the heavens.

Another stop was a ghost town with tell-tale signs of a hard-working community. We saw ruins of a saloon, a jail, a bed and breakfast, a mine, and even a closed-down post office. No ghosts. Everyone was gone.

Famous for burros walking unrestricted on the streets was an old mining settlement in Oatman, AZ. While strolling along, a mule got spooked and knocked my mom to the ground. *What happened to my protectiveness?* I was startled and ran from the scene. Feeling guilty, I sensed Joey, my invisible friend, abruptly demanding for me to have courage.

After that incident, I became Mom's bodyguard; no animal bigger than me could come near her. From being anxious to mellow to macho, I developed in maturity.

We also visited underground caves. *There were no trees for me to mark— strange place.*

Throughout our travels and upon reaching our destination, I was glad Mom didn't forget about Mexican food. *Why? I grew up with salsa, and it was my comfort food. Of course, it was followed by a cool bowl of water.*

As my lifestyle in New Jersey settled, experiencing an environment with four changing seasons was confusing. Insects, fleas, and ticks were new to me. In the hot weather, I had to remove my favorite sweaters. Then, it was cold. The weather here couldn't make up its mind. My daily walks in a wooded park with other dogs were the only consistent thing. Socialization with canines followed, but my protection of Mom continued.

Clinging to her around the clock, she assures me I am the joy of her life. I comfort her like a stuffed teddy bear comforts a child, only I have a heartbeat. *Who do I thank for my wonderful life? Joey? Mom? Or maybe Providence?*

Next: Some features from Randy's RV trips.

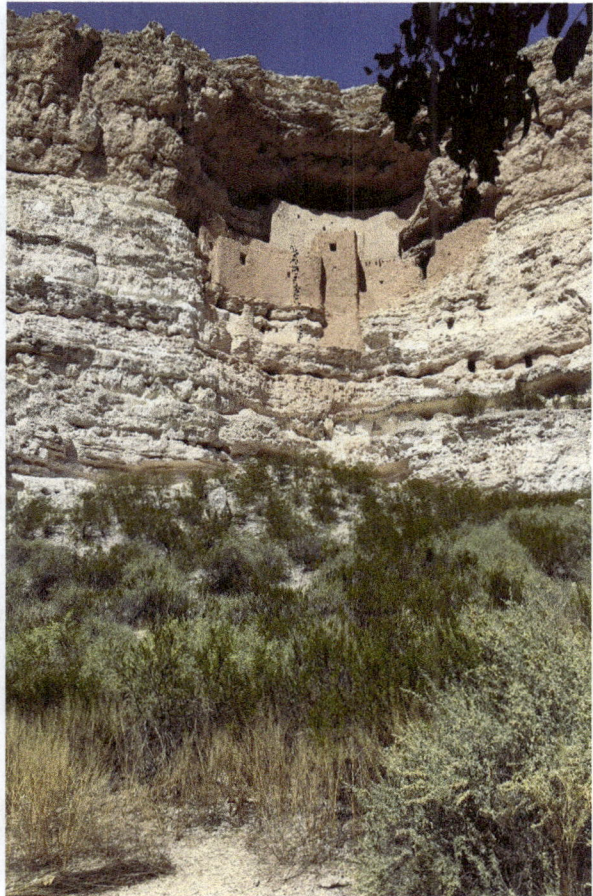

The mines, jailhouse, and saloons were empty. *Where are the Ghosts?*

There were no Indians to be found at Montezuma's Castle.
Did I scare them away, too?

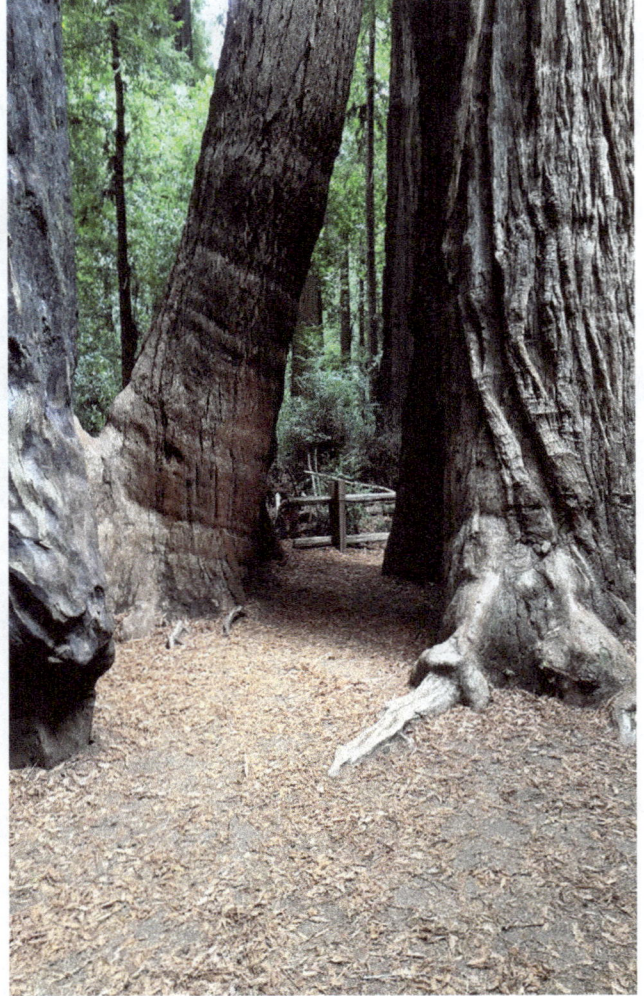

This huge tree was a great pit stop when I got off the train in the forest.

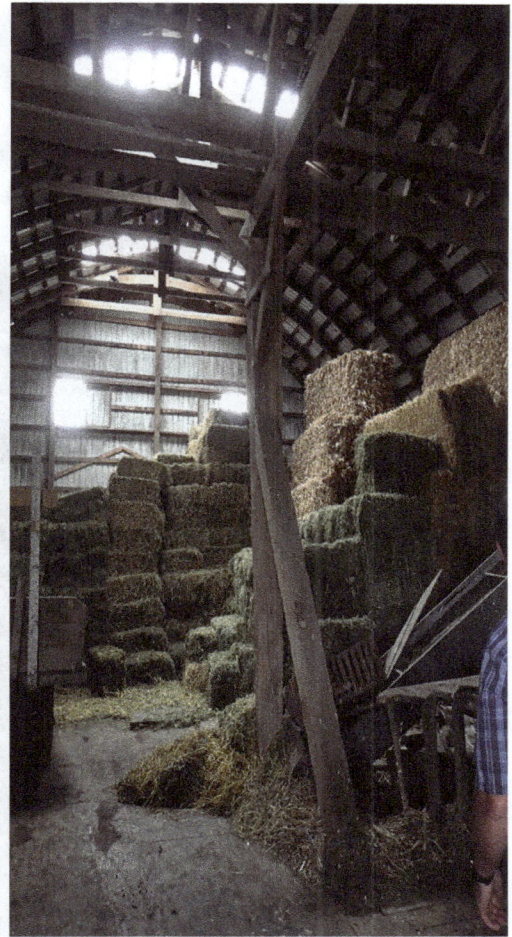

The horse and buggy ride brought me to an Amish Barn.
I was not permitted to climb the hay stacks.

The strangest place of all is Luray Caverns, Virginia. Pictured is something called "two fried eggs". *Definitely overcooked and hard as a rock.*

A rest stop in
Abilene, Texas.

*This was the most
luxurious pit stop ever.*

The sign read:
Canine Comfort Station

Seeley

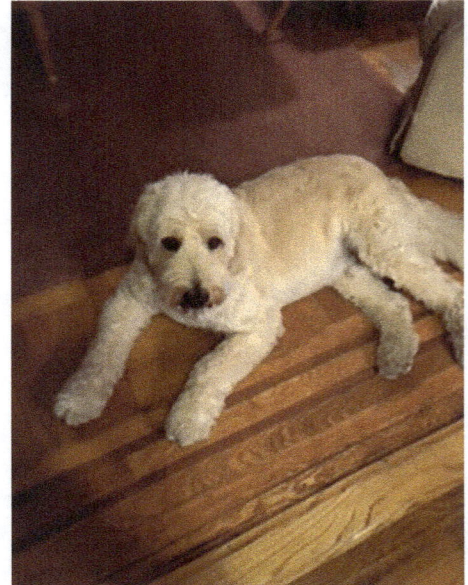

At eight weeks old, I left the breeding kennel and was adopted by a couple who wanted a Goldendoodle. *What made me special?* The gentleness of a Golden Retriever and the intelligence of a Poodle suited them. I was named *Seeley* after a family grandfather who loved dogs.

Kennel living to city living turned out to be an adventure. A tall building in Brooklyn, NY, where I took up residence, had lockers called elevators. Going up and down in these windowless cages with magic sliding walls led me to the great outdoors.

The ground-level entry didn't provide much freedom to run in open spaces. Leash walking with my new family did satisfy my sniffing opportunities to monitor the markings of neighborhood dogs. Fire hydrants and trees were regular stations.

With traffic and horns blowing, passersby spoke loudly and appeared in a hurry. I couldn't catch what they said, but Mom and Dad assured me they were not talking to me. People watching, with the expectations of more attention, confirmed I must have been handsome and an elite city dog.

From urban streets to the smell of salt water was the Jersey shore. Even though the trip between NY and NJ was only a jaunt over the bridge, heavy car traffic created delays in reaching our destination.

In New Jersey, our vacation home had an open deck to sunbathe. An elongated lounge chair perfectly accommodated my stature to stretch, relax, and keep an eye on the swans as they floated in the bay. Sitting on the picnic table made people see me better as they waved to me from their boats. Once I recognized them, I became the block security dog.

Having a private fenced-in yard, the "catch me if you can" game kept me and my dad on our toes. Being at the shore was a real bonus.

After several round-city/shore trips, the dead giveaway was seeing the ice chest cooler get filled with goodies. Once again, travel time. I always needed to decide which place I liked best.

Mom and Dad fancied holidays. The local city pet store invited the Easter Bunny in the spring and Santa Claus in the winter. Having my picture taken with a giant white rabbit was acceptable, but I had outgrown my belief in Santa Claus. Bunnies were real, as I have seen them hopping through grassy areas, but doubts crept in about Santa and his sleigh. *Why? They were hidden while I was sleeping.* Stuff toys were gifts from Mom and Dad, not Santa's make-believe bag, which was also hidden.

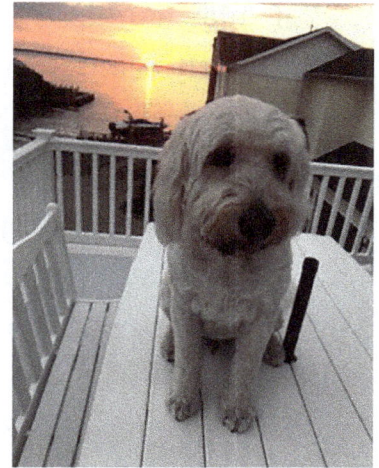

53

Soft play animals were plentiful, and upon examination of each of them, I meticulously removed the squeakers. The openings I made were with precision and left no apparent scars. Mom referred to me as being a "surgeon." Soon, I ran out of patients.

There were plush toys on Mom and Dad's bed, but they had no surgical needs and were not subject to my inspection.

Dogs bark to say something, and I'm no exception. To get out my whole story, I barked loudly. The dogs and animals on TV paid no attention to my speaking. *Were they not listening?* Mom did her best to explain that TV viewing differs from being in person, like the loud voices on the streets to overcome traffic noise. In frustration, when she couldn't hush me, my behavior was chalked up to emulate a "poodle personality."

Failure to cease barking did have its rewards. Mom bribed me with the words, "What does Mama have for you?" The gentleness of the Golden Retriever responded, and I gladly accepted the tempting treats. I got away with eating these snacks in bed, promising not to leave any crumbs.

Another road trip, this time not NY to NJ. It was a ten-hour excursion in a new car. Mom and Dad enjoyed the ride in the comfort of luxurious captain-styled seats. The passenger rear spaces were designed in a similar fashion. *Did they forget I was a dog?* I couldn't find any way to get comfortable. Unable to stretch out, my legs cramped. This was not a family car.

A sigh of relief came after one month. My wonderful, guilty parents traded in their new car and replaced it with another one. The seating arrangement in the rear had a bench style perfect for me to stretch, relax, and sleep. I loved car rides again, but there was nothing like home sweet home.

Getting served good meals included bacon, ground beef, rice, and buttered rolls. For dessert, homemade apple pie crust or lemon meringue pie caused me to lick my chops. People's food appealed to me more than generic dog food.

I love being spoiled. Any affection between Mom and Dad creates competition, calling me to butt in. Oh well, I've learned, it's OK. There's plenty of love to go around. Lucky me.

Samantha

I was born in the farming country of Lancaster, Pennsylvania. Adopted by an elderly lady, she provided me with a cardboard box, which didn't take long for me to trample down the sides, climb out, and escape. It was fun because she couldn't chase after me, as she declared, "Samantha, I have bad knees." My energy became too much for her, and I was assigned to the care of a dog sitter. The old lady was glad to get rid of me.

There were no boxes at the sitter's home to confine me. With lots of attention, I fell in love with this temporary home. Stubbornly, I made it evident to be re-adopted and not return to the "old lady's" broken-down bed box. After I overheard numerous discussions about what to do with me, my dog sitter and her husband opened their doors permanently.

Not behaving like a lady, I tended to be a "tom-boy," so my formal name of *Samantha* was shortened to *Sammy*.

A large yard at my new home allowed me freedom even though I was attached to a twenty-foot chain. That was heaven to me. A second heaven entered my life when I made acquaintances with other dogs at an off-leash park.

One of my new-found friends invited me to their home for a play date. *How many heavens are there?* Unfortunately, while visiting my buddy's home, I embarrassed my mom and climbed onto the kitchen table. *I experienced one less heaven. I got scolded.*

Playing with Mom at home was a bonus. Thinking it was okay to be rough and tumble around, I pulled on Mom's shirt and vigorously shook my head to score at tug-of-war. Oh no, unintentionally, I tore her clothes. *Would I get scolded again? Would I get disciplined?* I waited for an outcome, but none happened.

When Mom and Dad went on vacation, that saddened me. Prior scoldings confirmed that being left behind with a dog sitter was my punishment. Memories of earlier days surfaced, and I hoped there'd be no cardboard boxes to sleep in. It was like my life went in reverse. Unhappy…to happy…to depressing. I had to figure out how to make my parents feel guilty when they left without me.

As I lay in front of the glass sliding door, I focused on the activities of squirrels and birds. As if a light bulb went off in my head, my pining turned into an uncontrolled urge, and the perfect solution motivated me. I chewed up the kitchen linoleum floor and dug a hole through the plywood to get outside. Doing destructive things while they were not home assured me I would never be left behind again.

On their return, another scolding. While eavesdropping, I heard Mom tell Dad that this old house needed a new kitchen floor anyway and that Sammy had helped them decide more quickly to replace the flooring. *Was I in their good graces?* Still trying to figure it out.

Dog heaven returned. On the next vacation, I went with them. The beaches at the Jersey shore allowed me to swim to my heart's content. The only thing was that seaweed made me stinky, but I still loved it.

Mud puddles provided me with another dirty-stinky fun time. Being a Catahoula-leopard dog, bred to herd wild boar, gave me the excuse to run and roll in the mire.

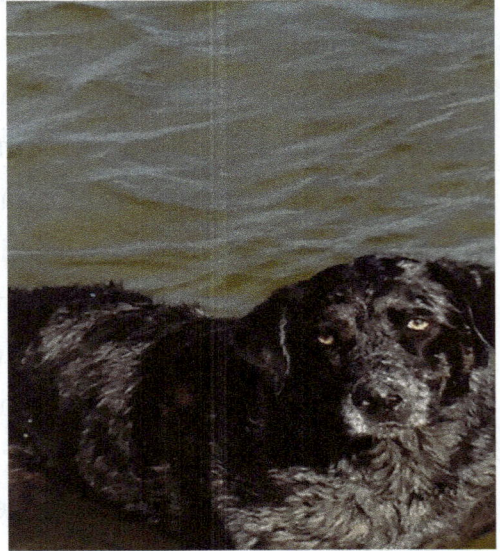

Problem solved. No more being excluded. No more dog sitters. I made my point. Hooray for vacations.

One day, while visiting a cemetery, where it was "deadly quiet," Mom wanted to experience a heartwarming, memorable person in her life. Surprisingly, a deer popped out of nowhere from the background wooded area. Immediately, I broke loose from the leash and chased after it, which caused Mom to fall flat on the ground. Guilt overwhelmed me as I returned to her side and licked her hand. It was my way of telling her I was sorry. All was forgiven; back to paying respects silently. The deer was no longer my priority. It was gone out of sight.

At my top weight of 80 lbs. I became a semi-retired "tom-girl" and gave up getting into mischief. Prolonged naps were a sure sign that slowing down was permanent.

Being grateful for a nice big bed reminded me of the days of living in a cardboard box, but thankfully, that was gone forever. The only thing that challenged my serenity was the cat that lived with me. I preferred not to share my bed. Otherwise, no complaints.

My life and my parents were great. They tolerated my behaviors, giving me many opportunities to experience many heavens on earth. Thanks.

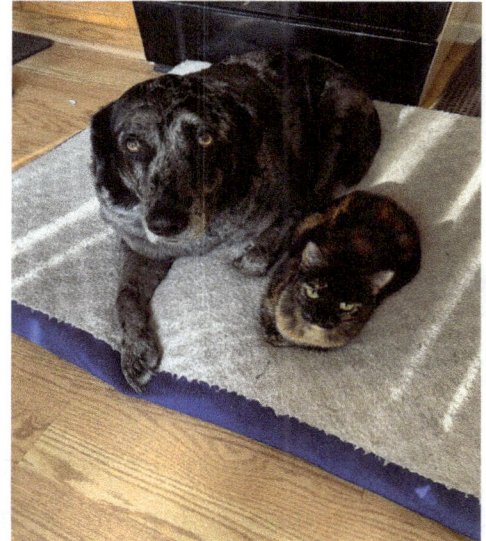

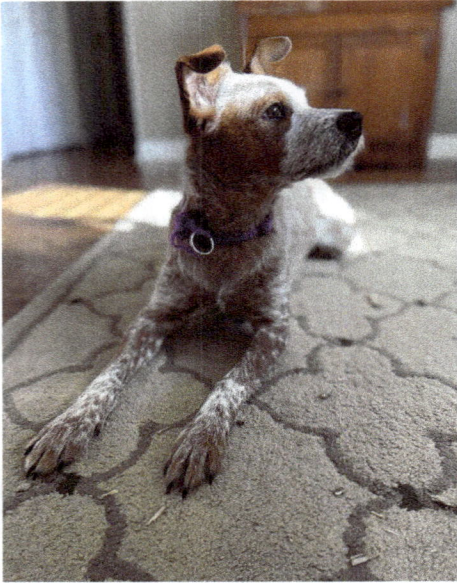

Roobee

My mama dog was a stray with no place to call home when she had a litter of puppies. A rescue team found us, and my siblings and I were separated one by one. Starting in Texas, my destination was New Jersey.

At two months old, I was ready to be adopted. Speckled orange/brown spots started appearing on my legs, identifying me as a red-heeler Australian Cattle dog. Inherent to my breed, I herd large groups across long distances and rough terrain by nipping at the ankles and legs of cattle and sheep.

With that ability, I picked out my new mom. Her ankles attracted me. She devised a name to embellish my native country: *Roo,* where kangaroos commonly reside, and with my fur coloring like a *Ruby* gem, my name was cleverly spelled out as *Roobee.*

It didn't take long for Mom's ankles to have multiple scratch marks on them. I played rough. With distractions of catching balls in mid-air, one right after another, I started to forget about her ankles. Perfecting my jumping skills, a fly could vanish in an instant.

Leash walking meant I had to adjust to domicile living. Fatigue was unheard of since I was trained to be a working dog. If I didn't want to go home, I'd throw a temper tantrum, like small children kicking and screaming until they got what they wanted.

Playing with other dogs didn't satisfy me. My uncouth mannerisms intimidated other canines, and their cowering response was no fun. Result: No dog friends.

Hanging around the house and staring out the window was a boring pastime. As a result of Mom's empathy, she decided to foster another dog named *Stella,* a six-year-old pit bull weighing eighty pounds. A Virginia resident claimed Stella couldn't get along with their farm goats, so she was dismissed as an unsuitable pet.

By welcoming Stella as a new housemate much bigger than me, Mom thought I could

be my rugged self, even if I were only thirty-five pounds. *If I could handle cattle, I could handle Stella.* Like siblings fighting in families, we were no different. We got into fights. That big girl developed anxiety. *Was I that dominating?*

Sharing Mom with Stella made me more attached to her side. If she sat on the sofa, I sat on one side of her and Stella on the other. In bed, Mom's middle position was sandwiched under the covers. Our body weights sealed the blanket nicely and tight. We had to ensure that she would not leave.

Was I an overly restrictive boss over Stella? Did Mom sense my governing control? A significant decision came about—no more residential living. Road travel for the next three years in a truck towing an RV motivated all of us. The words "buckle up" prompted us to hop into our personalized seats immediately. Off to the next destination, open living!

Sharing excitement with Stella, we discovered vacant lands, lakes, and snow, including surprises in meeting horses, hogs, and llamas. I expected Stella to improve her behavior during road trips, but no such luck. She continued to display apprehension, seeing strange farm animals. Being a cattle dog, ranch animals were natural to me. I had to protect her. Hanging out together in our RV and peering out the door was enough for Stella.

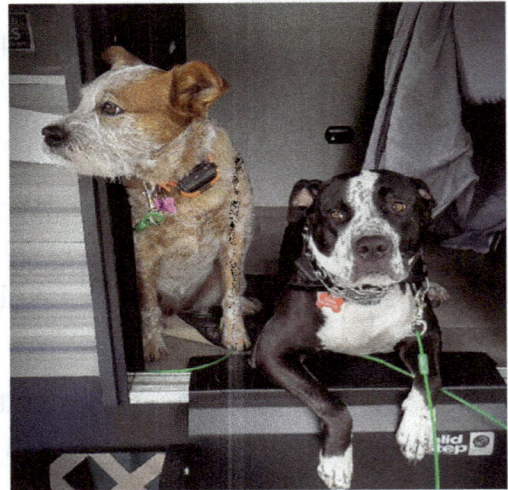

Exceptions occurred when she wandered by running off when no livestock was in view. I'd have to hunt for her—*bad girl.*

Outdoor living provided changes in our diets. I, Roobee, loved raw vegetables; Stella ate them by following suit. One of my favorites was Edamame beans, and I developed fine motor skills to shell them to get to the soybeans inside. For me, it was like a delicacy. For Stella, she'd attempt to eat the whole shell and bean, only to crunch them and spit them out of her mouth. *Lady-like, she was not.*

A treat we both loved was when Mom made frozen yogurt with berries. The ice cube tray made the perfect size for them to melt in our mouths.

Back to residential living - I forgot what that was all about. New indoor escapades are substituted for outdoor adventures. Finding *only* dirty socks in the laundry basket and burying them in house plants created missing pairs. Unfortunately, digging in the dirt made a mess that gave away my hiding places. I couldn't blame that on Stella. She was more sophisticated and refused to participate since she respected Mom's stuff.

I've gotten used to having Stella as my friend, but we still fight occasionally. I try to understand her anxiety, but my compassion hasn't been perfected yet.

Mom diligently observes the dynamics between us. Sometimes, she comforts our relationship by making a game out of unrest, laughing, and playing with us. That makes our tails wag, and all is good again.

Luckily, I don't bite Mom's ankles anymore. That's reserved for Stella's legs, and she finally got used to it. After all, I am a cattle dog, and that's what I do. I'm still bossy over Stella. Changing our loving home is not an option—friendship and love rules.

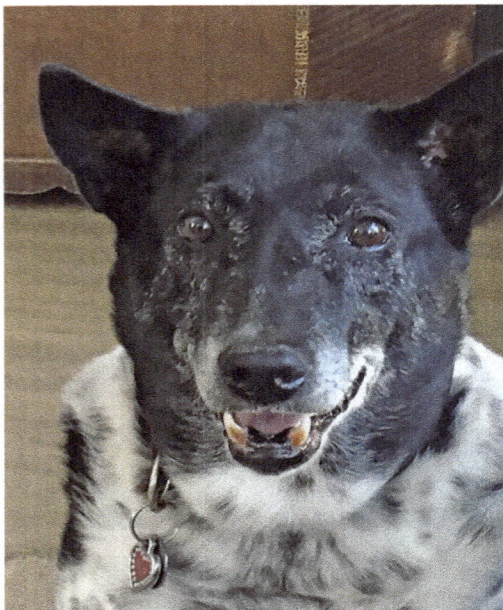

Ellie

Being a Soi dog in Thailand, living free-range on the streets was the only lifestyle I knew. After several litters and limited nourishment, sickness came along with the territory. Having Lyme disease and parasites, I was close to collapse and was dognapped by an organized gang, taken to a "dog meat trader," and named Elin DMT.

(*Aside: The countries of China and Vietnam pursue this as a legal business.*)

Hundreds of dogs were confined in cages at the dog meat holding centers where my interception occurred. Someone came and rescued several other dogs and me. *Now, where was I going*? In a warehouse, food was provided without having to hunt for it. Receiving medical attention gave me the will to survive once again. However, I lost my front teeth from malnutrition.

Next, I boarded an airplane to another unknown destination, traveling over eight thousand miles to the United States of America. A rescue volunteer helped me transition. Upon arriving in a strange land, there was a language that I couldn't understand. Sadness, fear, and puzzlement painted my face.

No longer being labeled Elin, DMT, my name became *Ellie.* My adoptive family waited for me for weeks and looked forward to my arrival. *Who were they?* I'd soon find out.

My new home had a fenced-in acre of land, and being a Jindo mix cattle dog, I was accustomed to digging. This allowed me to explore and listen to the sounds of gophers in underground tunnels. Smelling to my heart's content gave me freedom but in a different way. Not to smell for survival but for pleasure.

Several months passed before I realized how much Mom and Dad supported me in ways I never knew existed. Trusting was still an issue, but they showed patience and empathy. There were no crates or cages. Several beds throughout the house provided choices for me that seemed like a fairyland.

Toys, what were they? I didn't know how to play with them. Bones satisfied me because they were familiar.

Having fresh vegetables and fruit, such as green peppers, cabbage, carrots, apples, and more, was a dream. No leftovers. No street market garbage.

Opening a can of dog food could wake me from a sound sleep. The smell confirmed it was mine. I had a dish to eat from instead of a knocked-over trash can with worries about finding something to eat.

With no front teeth, when I smiled, I looked unfriendly. However, my curled lips were a sure sign of being happy and accepted.

I overcame my health challenges by seeking attention. Being a cattle dog, herding my family and any children visiting was how I requested their companionship. *Pet me, pet me.*

During times when Dad was alone and sat to rest, I put my chin on his lap and stared up at him. Still learning a new language, hand gestures were the best way to communicate with me.

Grooming is a way Mom pampers me; as a female, she must think I must be primped up. Life in the USA was undoubtedly different from Thailand. Being a tough girl, I never had luxuries. Only with a bribe of treats would I consent to nail clipping.

As I've grown older, I call California home now. My role of being protective of my surroundings, family, and food seems natural, not just for existence, even though memories have remained. With firsthand trust created by Mom and Dad, I have grown to be patient and lovingly affectionate. That's my survival story, and I am grateful.

Cletus Jenkins
a/k/a Cletus "T-bone" Jenkins

From a rescue center to a home, I was adopted by a young college student and given the name *Caramel* to describe my sweet puppy personality. Apartment living was too small to provide optimal space for a muscular male terrier mix, projected to weigh 85 lbs. My owner was confronted with a choice: to keep me contained in the small apartment or find me a new home. There was too much competition: educational studies vs. providing for a dog. I was no longer a priority.

An unexpected opportunity occurred to move to the country. The fresh air was so refreshing. I was more than willing to depart from tenement housing.

My new home had another dog living there who had a full-time job protecting the ranch. As a youngin, playing was more important than safeguarding. *Did I have to follow in the footsteps of this dog, referred to as the Sheriff?*

Intruders to keep under control were groundhogs, rabbits, birds, and squirrels, and they aspired to take over the corral. This called for adding a deputy, and I was turned into a genuine country dude with an appropriate name change: *Cletus "T-bone" Jenkins.*

My sniffer training began with my dad dropping carrot treats in the surrounding fields. These scavenger hunts sharpened my skills, and after proficiency, it was official: the old dog retired.

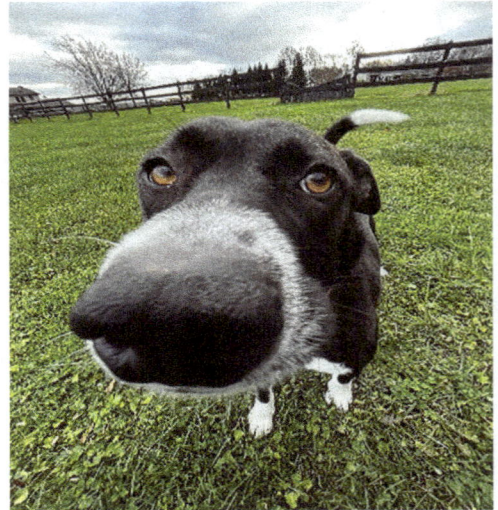

*There's a new Sheriff in town.
Beware critters.*

One day, a charming female guest dog visited via the plains. It was love at first sight, and a Calico Queen, she was not. My sweet "Caramel" heart had a pitter-patter and hoped we'd be friends for life. Sadly, her visit was temporary, and as she departed in the stagecoach, my short-lived dream created permanent memories.

I returned to keeping up my exhausting duties as I circled the ranch. Groundhogs have been insistent, returning like bandits among the willows. It stirred up an endless appetite.

Regarding chow time, Dad called out, "Want your porridge?" It's more than a soft, grainy meal. My dad, the chief chef at a saloon and gathering place, chopped up taters, veggies, and beef, mixing everything together. After I licked my lips from his belly-filling stew, Dad knew everything had passed the test to add to the menu. As the taste lingered, there was no comparison to any dry food. However, I'm glad Dad remembered I am a dog; rawhide chews were dessert treats for the Sheriff.

After ten years of keeping the peace, I told Dad it was time to hire an additional deputy to lighten up my load. As an elder, my interests have motivated me to climb onto Dad's lap to cuddle frequently. It's guaranteed. He won't move on the sofa with my total weight stretched over him. All my love and attention has gladdened his heart.

Dad started planning my retirement shindig as Sheriff. I reminded him that a new deputy would need my training to sharpen any intuitive skills and, of course, learn from the best "T-bone" in town,

While daydreaming about my puppy days, I practiced what it might be like to be fully retired. I remembered when Dad and I played together. With endless energy, I sprinted across the acreage, retrieved balls one after another, and hurried back for another round. In the cold winter of my first snow experience, I leaped into the air and caught a snowball, only to have it burst in my mouth. It was like drinking ice water while jumping in mid-air.

As I slowed down, my sleeping bunk was exchanged to be on the floor next to Dad's quarters. We used to sleep together.

My life had a real purpose with dual roles: gentleness and firmness. Most importantly, love, gratitude, companionship, and loyalty. I am confident that Dad will extend an unfeigned welcome to another new sheriff when the time comes. I so much looked forward to showing a newcomer all the ropes. However, after a deep sigh, time stepped in, and I was called to cross over the bridge.

The gopher stomping grounds patrolled by Sheriff Cletus "T-bone" Jenkins

Lola

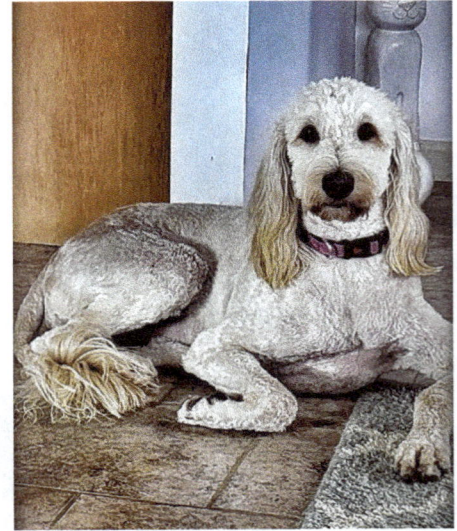

A couple drove three hours to bring home a Goldendoodle. Their minds and hearts were prepared for an apricot male puppy. Dishes and bedding were imprinted with the name Jake. However, there was no Jake. Faced with a decision, they didn't want to drive home without a dog. I became a second choice, a blonde female. Many names were tossed out. It took almost the entire ride home before I was named *Lola*. Goodbye to Jake's stuff. *Will they personalize a dish for me?*

I was accepted and invited to go everywhere with my new parents. By the time I was eight weeks old, I became a seasoned shopper.

One day, when I was at a store greeting customers, they started laughing and pointing fingers at me. Quickly, my dad turned around and responded to laughter. I couldn't resist the temptation to slip my head into a boa with blue, yellow, red, and green feathers, which caught everyone's attention.

Dad immediately called my name, Lola, to distract me. Someone started singing the lyrics about Lola, the showgirl (a Barry Manilow song)[1]. I was a temporary

---

[1] Copacabana (At the Copa). 1978. Original music from Barry Manilow. Lola was the showgirl in the lyrics. Copyright permission requested. No response. Refer to YouTube to play music.

showgirl, but Mom and Dad assured me that's not how I got my name. It was a nice tune, though.

On another shopping spree, I found a small pink pig that oinked. I couldn't resist that temptation and carried that toy in my mouth. Holding it tightly to the check-out register, I stood up with my front paws resting on the counter. The clerk scanned the item, and I made my first official purchase. It only took five minutes of satisfying pleasure to rip it apart.

When I go for walks and hear the sound of an airplane, stopping and staring upward into the sky keeps my attention until it disappears. Dad taught me the word "airplane." The helicopter is my favorite.

On our churchyard walks, I enjoy the wildlife. If there's a rabbit, I'll freeze in my tracks, but if there's a squirrel, look out! I'll chase it up the tree.

Garbage trucks hypnotize me. I want to observe all the processes of lifting and bringing cans down.

Being curious about everything, it's no wonder Dad and I walk about seven miles daily.

I discovered a swimming pool with another dog on one of my playdates. You guessed it. My friend and I jumped in, but it wasn't what we expected. There was a cover over the water. Call it a miracle; we walked on water! We never did find out if we got into trouble.

An opened door in our backyard room invited me to investigate. Fishing rods and hooks were hanging up. Since I had my own life jacket when boating, checking out the rods would satisfy my curiosity. Being discovered as missing, I patiently waited. It felt like hours until Dad found me with a fishing hook in the web of my paw. I was helplessly stuck but didn't cry for help. Dad, my hero, saved me by clipping the hook and ever so gently removing it. I healed quickly. Once again, I'm still trying to find out if I got into trouble.

My idea of comfort around the house is to delve into the laundry basket, selectively searching for Dad's socks and Mom's bra. They have the perfect scents to confirm that I'm never alone. The remainder of the clothes in the basket are tossed all over the floor. I guess I'm spoiled. I didn't get scolded.

I'm a picky eater and often don't eat as regularly as my parents think I should. Cooked meals, I may pass up. Offerings of peanut butter cookies and ice cream don't capture my fancy. My favorite treats, I won't turn down, are duck jerky and a double order of bacon at a restaurant. My mom thinks I'm trying to keep my girlish figure. I weigh 65 lbs.

I love and care for my mom and dad like they love and care for me. My dad had a health challenge and told me I was his life-saving therapy dog. Mom tells me I comfort her. *Does that make me an emotional support dog?* Even though I have several roles, most of all, I want to be cherished as their unconditional companion. They often say, "I make their house a home," but I'm the one who's grateful they adopted me.

Oh, by the way, I'm not the second choice anymore. I'm Number One. The name Lola now identifies what belongs to me.

Chance, Tucker, and Lola

Park Executive Committee Meeting

**The rules: What happens at the Dog Park
stays at the Dog Park.**

Champ

I don't know where I came from, but I soon found out where I was going. A wonderful couple took me in, and not long after that, I received lots of attention. My name, *Champ,* remained unchanged, which helped me feel secure. Wow! Their home was great! I'm not bragging, but I had it made.

I'd sit on the dock in the early mornings by the water and watch the ducks float by as they discussed their day.

Wanting to please my new dad, he'd call me to come and sit beside him. With my eyes closed and head tilted downward, he'd kiss my forehead. Embarrassed, I pretended I wouldn't say I liked it, but I did. It took some time before I gave up my submissive mannerisms and developed a macho attitude to request kisses by giving him my paw.

It was time to learn a trick. When Dad put a cookie to rest on my nose, he demanded I sit like a statute. With the action word, "OK," I flipped the cookie in the air, precisely catching it. Dad's happy face lit up with pride. It was an easy task to learn.

One of my favorite places to visit was my uncle's eighty-acre homestead. After several walks around the perimeter, where I could run off leash, I learned the boundaries. I was smart that way.

On "leash only" restricted walks, I fetched my lead from the hook on the wall and carried it in my mouth. No collar, no restriction. I complied with the rules, but my way. *Rules, rules, everywhere rules. What happened to my decision-making freedom?* That's why I liked my trips to visit my uncle.

When my dad retired, I started going everywhere with him. Places included lumber yards, hardware stores, and marinas to get bait for fishing. Anywhere was OK if I could be with him. I loved being his shadow.

With my reserved seat in his van, others knew I didn't share. No questions were asked. However, I couldn't understand why I had a special seat with Dad but couldn't have my chair or sofa in the house. That was Mom's rule. If I was left alone, I climbed into their bed, hoping they wouldn't figure it out. Somehow, they knew.

Realizing I was a boxer who drooled, Mom was ready with a towel; my face got wiped frequently. I thought she was playing a game with me. Every time she mopped my face, I got a smile and "Good boy."

Keeping me groomed was a chore. I got dirty often. I showered with Mom. That I liked. The warm water was far better than going out in the rain or being squirted with the hose.

Even though Mom made sure she served me good food, I hoped tasty table handouts would drop my way. That never happened.

Learning that Mom and Dad had different rules taught me diplomacy. Dad and I went places together, played, and had fun. Mom was strict, probably because she had to discipline six children. When none of the siblings lived at home anymore, I became the youngest one in the family.

I lay in front of the fireplace with my blanket during the winter months. Sometimes, I'd carry my blanket to my dad to cover me. Being a great guy, he knew just what I wanted.

Lying around was not my forte, but it happened as I grew older. I felt extra tired and wasn't my perky self. I needed a check-up. Everyone at the vet's office was friendly, so I didn't mind going. Questioning why I went to three visits in one day, which included a specialist, bewildered me. The only understanding I had was that my physical exhaustion was unrelenting. My spirit heard the vet say, "Champ had a heart attack." It saddened me that Mom and Dad would lose our companionship. We spent 11 years of fun, adventure, joy, and love. Great memories were made during our lifetime together.

My name, Champ, suited me well.

As time passed, Mom joined me. She frequently whispers in Dad's ear, "He was our champion dog."

View from across the bridge
Freedom Fields County Park, Little Egg Harbor, NJ

Otis

I was born on the beautiful island of Puerto Rico by the Caribbean Sea. As a six-week-old puppy, my life became confusing when my only comfort was with my mom, brothers, and sisters, which soon ended. In September 2017, the forceful winds of Hurricane Maria knocked out all the power, and the pounding rain flooded our home. I couldn't find my family and was left behind, alone, and terrified.

Rescue workers found me shaking and provided me with food and shelter. A nasty, unrelenting, itchy rash developed on my belly from being wet and dirty.

The storm passed, and I survived the experiences I will never forget.

Where was I going? Sounds and rumbles added to my nervousness as an attendant put me into an airplane crate. I traveled over a thousand miles to the Atlantic City Humane Society[1] and woke up in an unfamiliar shelter with many dogs. Tides changed, and I considered myself a lucky puppy. I got adopted and was named *Otis*.

My new mom fell in love with me, and her caring touch gave me the security I needed. Dad had a busy lifestyle, which meant unexpected changes for him.

---

[1] Humane Society of Atlantic County, Atlantic City, NJ. Private non-profit organization.

Being a male pit bull mix with lots of energy, a trainer helped to teach me basic commands, which came quickly. Given a place on the rug called "my spot," it was a comfortable bed with a warm blanket - *my sanctuary.*

Mom found out that baths would make me shake. *Please - no water - no rain.* The hurricane traumatized me. Refreshing water when I get my teeth brushed was acceptable.

Discovering toys kept me busy, and carrying two tennis balls in my mouth made me like a chipmunk. Spiky-type balls that squeak became my favorite.

On Memorial Day, Dad took me to the beach with my plastic spiky ball, and we played catch together for hours. Even though the wet sand clung to the spikes, I didn't mind the gritty feeling in my mouth. Swallowing too much sand made me very sick.

Lying there lifeless, as if I was no longer for this world, I thought, *could this be my Memorial Day?* The emergency visit to the vet revived me with intravenous fluid, which wasn't pleasant, but seeing my mom and dad's faces was the best medicine, and that brought out a sense of fortitude in me. I returned home lovingly pampered, and needless to say, I had extra teeth brushing to get rid of the grit between my teeth.

My spiky ball continues to remain my favorite. When I bring it to the dog park and roll it back and forth in the grass, I can retrieve it without fear of any connection to that memorable beach day. At least, I thought, no fear.

One day, my ball fell into a gopher hole, so I dug and dug deeper and deeper. No find. *Did I lose my ball?* My perseverance terminated when daylight turned to dusk, and it was time to go home. Mom understood my dismay and gave me a new spiky ball. Thanks, Mom. I became the protector of my new possession.

I have a good appetite. Chicken, eggs, and cheese satisfy me. The smell of cheese can lure me out of a sound sleep. I also like a salad with meals: lettuce, carrots, and celery.

Cooking smells tempt me. After all, I am a dog. Mom was making Irish Soda bread for a holiday celebration, and without her closely watching me, I snatched the loaf off the counter along with a batch of raisins and ate them. I intended it to be a secret tale, but it didn't turn out that way. Since raisins can be toxic in dogs, I was rushed to the vet again.

A count of thirty-one raisins was pumped out of my cramping, upset stomach by the vet. Fortunately, I had no other side effects. After that encounter, the clinking sounds of pans and dishes remind me not to get too anxious when Mom is baking despite great smells.

When Mom and Dad's grandpa and grandson visit, I cry excitedly and want to lick their faces to greet them. Running in circles with "the Zoomies," even though I think I am a mellow guy, my enthusiasm comes to the surface like a fast thoroughbred.

Grandpa refers to me as the "RCA Victor Dog."[2] *Who was that dog? Will I ever meet him?* No such luck. That dog was from an old memory Grandpa had many decades ago.

---

[2] The iconic image of a terrier-mix dog, Nipper, looking into a phonograph became an international symbol of quality and excellence for the Victor Talking Machine Company and later RCA Victor. Established in 1901, Camden, NJ.

Several years have gone by, and Dad's retired now. He gives me his full attention, and I hear him tell Mom, "I can't imagine life without Otis." As for me, I can't imagine life without them. Mom and Dad understood my ordeal, and I love them for saving me. They've provided me with a new home I never thought was possible.

Some may say I'm lucky to have overcome several hurdles. My past has resulted in developing a newfound character, including confidence and gratitude. *Yes, that does make me a lucky boy!*

Not yet. Keep walking.

Stella

It was a long trip from El Paso, Texas, where I first lived. At least I didn't travel alone, mistaken for German Shepherds; my brother and I were transported to a humane society in California.

Many dogs occupied several cages, impatiently waiting for the right person to take them home. The kennels were noisy, but I didn't contribute to the demands of other dogs. Choosing not to bark, I attracted attention and received a play date in a large outdoor pen. Without hesitation, my paws touched a lady's chest and shoulders, and I selected her as my new mom. It was like I proposed to her, and she accepted. Coming from an ethnic family, she wanted to give me her favorite Italian female name: *Stella.* After a few months, I started to learn Italian words.

My distinctive identity as a Mountain Cur breed was revealed when I was about a year old. Having a brindle coat with striations and turned-down ears, compared to the sharply stand-up ears of a German Shepherd, I was reclassified.

Even though I did my best to adapt to living with a stay-at-home mom, she wanted me to have outside activities. My uncle filled those shoes. Explorations to various parks perked up my intrinsic need for the outdoors. *That's amore.* (Love).

Not everyone was my friend, whether human or dog. With a keen sense of someone's disposition, my inborn temperament escalated my awareness.

One day, while playing at the park with friendly dogs, a muscular-eighty-pound Doberman, almost double my weight, barged into our pack and decided to be the dominant dog. With the command from my uncle, *Abbastanza* (Enough), I needed help to obey. My courageous instinct as a fighter forced me to step up to the plate and watch over my playmates. That was a real test of my determination; the physical battle was on.

Frightened on-lookers screamed! It was like a ring with no time-outs. Over the growling and barking, my uncle became our referee. He took control and shouted out my name, **STELLA**! With hair standing up on both our backs and panting, the fight was called. Leashes were attached to our harnesses, and our masters forcefully pulled us back to our corners. There were no injuries except our respective feelings of pride.

Someone at the park asked if Stella got her name from the movie *Streetcar Named Desire.*[1] There was a famous scene where Marlton Brando called out frantically, "**Stella!**" No connection. No further questions.

---

[1] "Streetcar Named Desire." 1951 Warner Bros. movie.

Crossed paws like a lady in the quiet comforts of home, Mom concealed me as "a fatal blossom." The encounter with the Doberman was the telling tale.

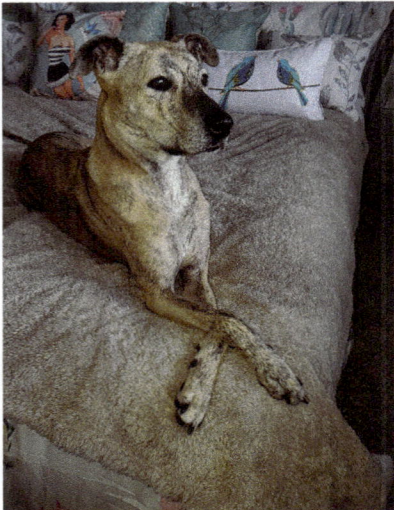

After that park incident, my priority to protect my home peeked, and I became interested in possums, geckoes, and crows. My couch-like bed was strategically placed by a door with perfect outside views. With my presence known, intruding critters were warned to seek a fast, amicable escape. When everything was quiet and under control, I told myself, *good job, Stella*, I let out a sigh of relief with a smile on my face. *Peace be still.*

Often, a background of soft rock music played on the radio. Listening to one song, *"Lean on Me,"*[2] seemed to instruct me about what to do. *What was happening to Mom?* Detecting a sentimental tear in her eye, I needed to comfort her. Climbing up on the sofa, I stretched out my body and guided Mom to use my back as her pillow. *Rest your head, Mom.* My presence told her how much I loved her and that everything would be OK.

When Mom goes on errands, I'm a home-alone dog, like the boy in the movie *Home Alone.*[3] Trash cans get emptied and dragged to other parts of the house, bathroom toilet paper trails are left behind me, and pillows are tossed off the furniture. I'm obsessed with white plastic trash bags. *Why? I don't know.* When she

[2]   "Lean on Me." Released in 1972 by Bill Withers, singer, and songwriter.
[3]   "Home Alone" Release 1990 Walt Disney movie.

returns and sees what I've done, my ears droop. That's my way of apologizing. Understanding the stress of her absence, I'm forgiven, and peanut butter cookies comfort me.

Mom knows I have a tidy side. With a TV remote, cell phone, or a magazine lying on her bed or my bed, my nose goes to work and pushes them off onto the floor.

Reading her like a book, I know her every move, every emotion, and activity. She tells her friends about our mutual love and how she won the lottery when she took a chance to rescue me. I guess I was **thee** big ticket item, which turned out to be a **Win-Win!**

Ruby

Where I came from, I have yet to learn. *Was I lost?* Someone found me roaming in the woods and brought me to a shelter. Pictures of me were posted to find a roof over my head and have food to satisfy my emaciated body.

A little girl saw my photo and begged her parents to adopt me. The family already had two elderly dogs and hoped I'd make a good companion for them. Being a Pitbull/Staffordshire terrier mix turned out differently than expected. *Did I play too rough for the little girl?*

I was brought to another home and adopted by a couple who called me "Special Girl." Given the name *Ruby,* I filled their hearts with fun and laughter. I immediately bonded with my new family. There was no turning back when my previous owners begged that I be returned.

Being part of an active lifestyle, camping adventures included trail hiking. Mom liked to trample through the woods, while Dad chose to sleep in the tent to catch up on much-needed rest.

Off-leash freedom introduced me to a forest with puddles, swamps, and ponds. One memorable day, I saw a deer amongst the tall tree-filled branches. My curiosity peaked, so I followed the deer as it darted around a swamp. Taking a shortcut to avoid the trees, I sank quickly into the bog. Somehow, I paddled to reach a tree stump in the middle of the mire, barking to catch Mom's attention. Dad was summoned to my rescue, saving me from the consuming soggy wetland.

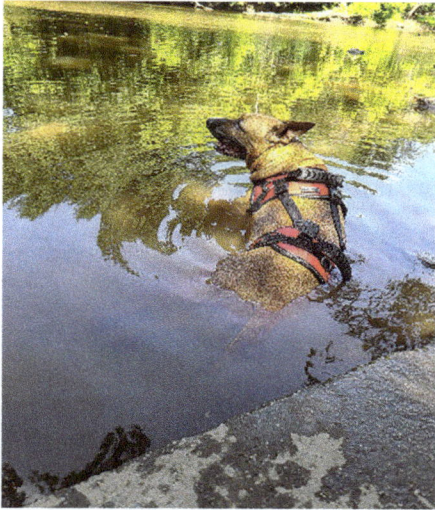

It became apparent that I had chosen the wrong path to chase after the deer, but the bog incident didn't deter my efforts. With a sigh of relief, Mom and Dad were relieved that I was back on the bank. However, with determination, I once again, with continued vigor, pursued after the deer, but this time, I leaped through the mud. At least I was not sinking. *What happened to the deer as it disappeared into the forest?* End of the hunt. Out of sight.

As a result of encounter number two, my four legs were covered in mud. Mom and Dad laughed to see my limbs painted in the deep brown sludge: "Ruby's wearing trousers!" *What next? How would I get into the car to return to the campsite with such gushy grime all over me?*

As if a light bulb had gone off over the heads of Mom and Dad, handfuls of leaves of all shapes and sizes, dry brown or soft green, were gathered. They rubbed all the mud off me and removed my "trousers." Embarrassing! I loved camping anyway.

My lack of agility around the house was humorous at first. It was chalked up as clumsy when I missed my mark jumping onto our sofa. There were incidents when I mindlessly wandered into a door jam. *Was I getting older and tired because my back limbs failed to keep up with the front part of my body?*

Was I reacting for attention to an unexpected turn of events in my domain? Was it my fault that Mom and Dad decided on a separation since they grew apart? Heaviness set in with sadness, and I became despondent. Being assured that I was loved, my parents decided to share my custody and created visitation rights.

Keeping up with frequent visits became a challenge. Walking became uneasy. Warming my legs with a heating pad for comfort was only short-lived. A wagon became my means of transportation. Seeing how restrictive this way of life was for me, my vet suggested a wheelchair. What a turn of events! Enthusiasm returned to my life.

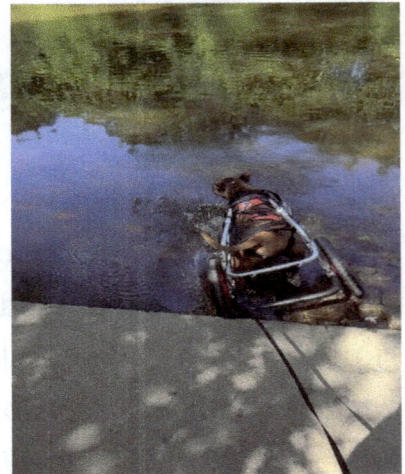

Hooray, I'm back to the great outdoors.! My dream of camping again came true. Mom took me to a site with rushing water, and it spoke to me. I forgot all about the wheelchair and plunged into the water, chair and all. Happiness filled me. It was my last camping trip.

My life was packed with adventure for eleven years, and I learned to overcome numerous challenges. My mom and dad clearly understood my "woo-woo" howling, which meant their love and support was gratifying. That's what life is all about.

I'm busy. Keep walking

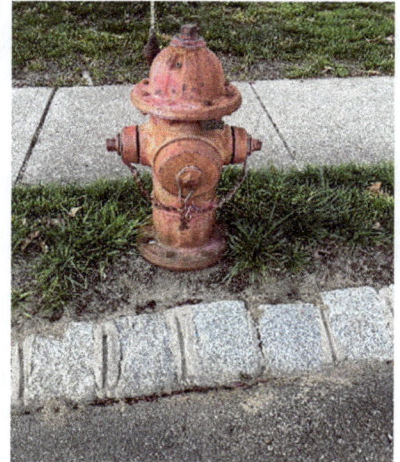

Murphy

As a puppy, I lived with a family unsuited for my lifestyle. As a Treeing Walker Coonhound, my reputation has been known to be stubborn. It was hard to train me unless I consented. Being a born raccoon hunter, chasing them up into trees was a way to ensure their safety from the speed and endurance of my breed.

I decided to escape from my original family because discipline was not for me. Being homeless, living on the streets, and fending for food wasn't the anticipated outlook, but being smart and brave, I somehow managed.

Did I give up freely? Unwillingly, remembering my capture, I was transported to a shelter in a large enclosed truck. A description from the Georgia Humane Society[1] gave me a AAA rating. Wondering: *Were they really describing me? I don't think so.* Off I went to New Jersey to an adoptive family who named me Murphy. My new mom wanted a good old Irish name.

---

[1] The Humane Society of Statesboro and Bulloch County, Inc. Georgia. A volunteer-based non-profit 501 (c)(3) organization saving pets since 1980.

Once again, living in a confined home was much different than roaming the streets. I couldn't just look out the window, longing for the outdoors, so I dismantled the Venetian blinds since they obstructed my view. Doing my best to stay occupied, I chewed the TV remote control; the furniture needed refreshing; the bed just for me needed fluffing up; the grandchildren's soft dolls were carried and torn apart; and toy trucks that moved across the floors were running away from me. Living in new quarters, many temptations forced me to burn pent-up energy.

I wanted to chew or eat everything in sight, including napkins, and my sweet tooth hunted out hidden candy. Now, I was labeled as Murphy, the glutton.

Hearing a stern voice from Mom, "We are taking you back to Georgia, where you came from," was an ultimatum. All the items I destructively transformed came from my lack of discipline as a street dog; no one was there to correct my conduct. Mom and Dad lost patience with me.

Begging for a second chance, a routine was started. Daily walks, ball playing, and being with other dogs helped me develop the necessary socialization skills.

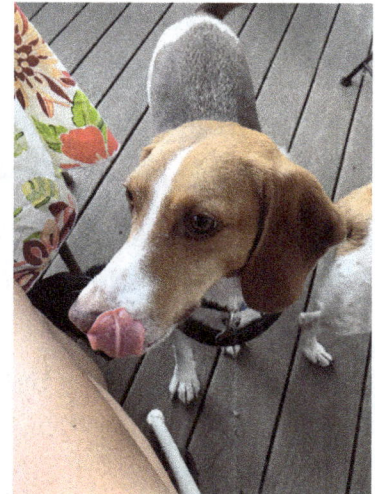

Chasing delivery trucks brought up bad memories. Progress, not perfection, has been my aim. After all, barking, a hound characteristic, was challenging to control.

A terrible change happened at home. One day, Mom was no longer with us. Maybe I will see her someday "across the bridge." Becoming Dad's best friend, our bonding improved my demeanor since we needed each other.

When going for car rides, Dad understands my limitations by bringing a bucket for me because I get car sick. Doing my best to control my upset stomach isn't a choice of mind over matter. Otherwise, I'd look forward to more travel outings.

We moved to another family home with Dad's daughter and her three dogs. Some of my old behaviors came back. As I attempted to steal food from the elder dog, the dogs that protected the senior immediately placed me in a lower rank. Excluding food, my new dog family exhibited kindness and allowed me to nap in their beds.

Christmas was an active time of year for my family. I couldn't resist opening wrapped packages. Dressing up like Santa Claus, Dad wasn't fooling me. The children laughed excitedly as they tugged on Santa's beard and received gifts. *Were they trying to find out if Santa was real or make-believe? Did he really come down the chimney?* Unanswered questions. Fun times.

Sometimes, it's hard to remember my street-living days. There were many challenges I had to overcome. When I put my paws on Dad's shoulder, and we look into each other, eye to eye, I feel like he has forgotten all the mischief I got into. I'm forgiven with love and acceptance. Sleeping beside him keeps me company. I'm grateful for second chances as I grow one-day-at-a time.

Jesse and Mia

While wandering on an empty road in Virginia, being lost, someone felt sorry for me, picked me up, and I ended up in New Jersey. A local newspaper read: *HELP WANTED. A one-year-old German Shepherd mix named Jesse is waiting for you. Please call your local shelter."* Weeks passed, but no one responded, so I was placed in a foster home.

One day, a lady was visiting her accountant's office when a conversation about an abandoned dog came up. This compassionate dog lover made a serendipitous decision, and I was adopted.

My new home had an open yard, but soon, a chain-linked fence was installed to accommodate my freedom when Mom had to work. The woods behind the house reminded me of my roving days. I dug a hole under the fence to investigate my new surroundings to prove I was an escape artist.

A loud siren led me to a firehouse at the end of the road. Being welcomed with treats from the volunteer men stationed there became my priority stop. Hanging out for hours, watching the big trucks go in and out of the garage, I volunteered my friendliness.

Another frequent stop of mine was at an inviting local creek. When I returned home covered with mud, Mom put me on probation with orders not to leave the house when she was working. To soften her mandates, she'd bribe me with pig ear treats, but I was still bored.

A small lost female dog appeared as I peered out the window, keeping my eyes fixated on the woods. Generally, I'm not too fond of other dogs. *Why I had an interest in her, I can't explain.* Alerting Mom, the local State Police was called to help find the owner. She was scanned for a chip, but none was found.

Another ad was placed in the local newspaper. *"FOUND. Lost female Pomeranian."* Luckily, the owner claimed her.

I daydreamed about that small dog named *Mia.* She showed up in the neighborhood again a few months later. After a night's sleepover, Mom diligently brought her back to her owner but was flabbergasted when the owner didn't want Mia anymore. Once again, Mom made a serendipitous decision to accept her as my companion. Wow! I didn't have to be bored or home alone.

Being a big brother gave me a sense of responsibility. I developed good habits, like staying home rather than performing disappearing acts.

With my keen sense of smell, Mia's teeth were a dead giveaway; she had bad breath. I didn't want her kisses, even though I liked her. Mom took action by visiting the vet, dentist, and groomer. All those necessities improved her general health, and after that, there were no restrictions on our companionship.

Grooming softened her fur, which convinced me not to play in the muddy creek. *Would grooming help me, too? Maybe.*

The one thing Mia did, which I didn't like, was steal my food. Mom had to solve the problem of where my bowl was placed so she couldn't reach it. But Mia found a way to jump up on the chair and steal Mom's food instead if she just turned her head. *She was a little devil, but I still loved her.*

Satisfied to keep each other company, our lives were simple. At night, we bedded down together in the same room. Sometimes, I'd sleep in her bed, even if it was too small.

Mia was my companion for over half of her life. She was thirteen when she left me, so I knew it wouldn't be long before we'd meet again. When I was fourteen, my heart was filled with joy when Mia greeted me as I crossed the bridge. Reminiscing about our memories together, we were grateful to have a loving, warm-hearted mom with an open door.

Charlie

I'm a mixed-breed male dog. An Alabama animal rescue team found me wandering through the woods. The scents of feral animals spurred me to investigate anything I could find for food. One of the workers named me *Charlie Brown*[1], after a cartoon character who sometimes appeared lost. The wilds were all I knew until the day I was found and brought to a shelter.

It was a long ride in an open pick-up truck, and being in a cage, I caught the refreshing breeze, unlike the still air of the forest. I ended up in New Jersey after my adoption. My new parents knew my struggles and wanted the best for me.

I was enrolled in daycare, but *what was daycare?* I found out it was a place where other dogs had a lavish lifestyle and went there two times a week to play, nap, and play again. I got used to that luxury that was so different from the thick growth of trees and underbrush. My name was shortened to *Charlie*," and the *Brown* disappeared from my character as I became confident. Perhaps that's why I had mixed feelings. Daycare or home? I loved both places.

---

[1] Charlie Brown is a character from the Peanuts cartoon. Permission is requested with no response.

Walking on days I didn't go to daycare, Dad and I had quality time. We walked here and there for about three miles. Afterward, Dad was tired, but I wasn't.

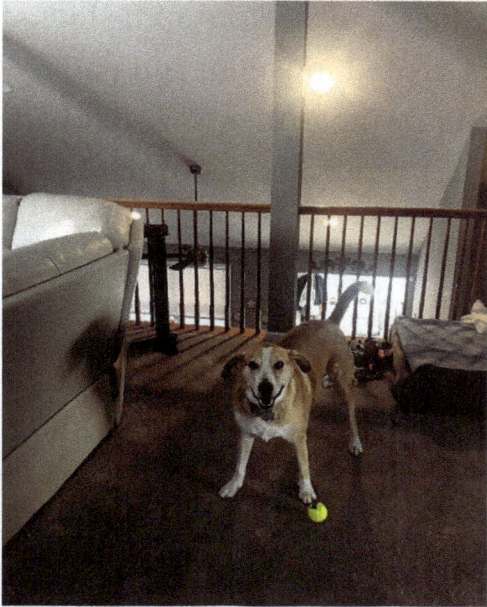

One day, while playing in my fenced-in yard, my curiosity got me into trouble. I broke a solar light, glass cut my paw, and I went to an emergency vet visit for stitches. Being handicapped for only a few days, living in the wilderness taught me survival skills. The pain was insignificant.

My home had an expansive loft with surrounding windows so I could see everything outside. The views appealed to me, so I decided to claim this vacant area as my kingdom. It was also the best place for me to be a guard dog and alert my family if anyone approached our home.

Playing with my squeaky toys that talked back and with a ball that ran away prompted me to find amusement during my alone time.

My parents noticed I started limping after climbing the steps. A vet confirmed there was a potential problem with my hip. *What kind of problem?* My mom and dad were concerned it might be arthritis. It never stopped me from going to my sanctuary; it was a minor challenge. After getting a new orthopedic bed, I was convinced that the loft belonged to me. The bed was placed near the railings at the top of the steps. Sleeping with one eye open and one closed allowed me to rest and keep a watch on the first-level living quarters.

Slowly, the loft area was filling up with a sofa and TV. Mom and Dad joined me for TV watching at the end of their day. Entertaining guests turned out to be lots of fun. That meant extra cookies and venison treats. I invited my mom and dad's grandchildren for sleepovers; now, people's beds are in my apartment. My flat had an open-door policy, except cats were not welcome; they reminded me of the squirrels in the wilderness, climbing on everything.

One of my favorite shows on TV was the Westminster Dog Show. I was captivated by the strides and focused attention of the show dogs. *Why did they not bark like I do?* On other programs, the dogs barked. I did my best to figure out my curiosity, but there was no resolution.

My mom and dad think I'm royal, but *how did I get that way?* They treat me like a king. From a wanderer who survived living in the forest, I never anticipated a life filled with love and compassion. I have everything I could ever need and more, including my rent-free apartment. I'm pampered, and I love it.

Capitola, CA
One of Randy's Casual Walks

I can't find any fire hydrants.

Willow

As a puppy, my first home was in Florida, where I lived for about two years. I was named *Willow* after the beautiful weeping willow trees surrounding the area.

Being an overly energetic female French Bulldog, my energy overwhelmed the family, who never owned a dog. Coming to my rescue, another member of the same clan with an active lifestyle embraced me and gladly accepted my unlimited vigor. I had the best of both worlds: visits to my first home and now residing with new adventurous parents.

I must admit that my life was confusing at first, but eventually, it became easier. There were two homes to live in: a winter home in Florida and a summer home in New Jersey. Traveling from place to place presented many adventures that suited my personality. I traveled by car or train on land and a boat at sea, but I wondered if I'd ever fly in an airplane.

Boating was fun. Watching the fish leap out of the water tempted me to jump in. It's a good thing I remembered I can't swim. Just in case I fell overboard, I wore a life jacket with my name and phone number. It identifies me as the first mate, even though Mom thought otherwise. Dad was the captain.

There were occasions when we'd stop at a dock for restaurant dining. My favorite food was a hamburger. I shared the bun with the seagulls. Mom and Dad usually had seafood dinners. If Dad caught fish while we were boating, we ate at home.

Casino visits were too much to comprehend with all the noises and flashing lights. Screams of excitement and laughter. from people's activities intrigued me. I wanted to know if I needed to be a guard dog or humbly witness all the happenings. Mom and Dad assured me that this was one of the ways others had fun. It wasn't my idea of jest, but being home alone wasn't an option.

Off-leash dog parks where I could socialize with other dogs, big or small, allowed me to run and be chased. I built up my running speed to 25 mph, hydroplaning through the air. My flat nose made it difficult to breathe after a hard run. Dad came to my rescue with a gallon jug of water. He poured it all over me, which cooled me off. I was back to being perfect again.

My mom's voice captivates me. I'll stop whatever I'm doing, turn my head in her direction, and eavesdrop on every word. I've learned to understand sentences.

I overheard a conversation Mom had on the phone with a friend. It sounded like plans to take me to a unique membership-only dog park in Lancaster, Pennsylvania. This dream place had hundreds of tennis balls that fell from the trees, fountains to splash in, tunnels to run through, and the greatest lawns to roll around in. I'm keeping my paws crossed that this will be a priority play date. If I ever get there, I'll pretend to be surprised.

Determined to go wherever Mom goes, I nap on her shoes and handbag. That's my clue that she is still at home. When she's resting, lying my head on her foot assures me of the closeness we have for each other. Dad, the activity parent, delegates all the adventures. They balance their lifestyle to include me: shopping, vacations, visits with family or friends, TV watching, you name it. I am their shadow, except for two off-limits.

At home, there's a sign on the door, "Caution, no entry to Willow." It's Mom's special room where she makes beautiful art from stained glass. It hurts my feelings that I can't be with her there, but slivers of glass might injure my paws. Even if I tip-toed with total awareness, I'm still not permitted entry. When Mom opens the door, I wag my short tail and stand up happily with only my back legs, and she rewards me for my patience with a treat.

The other off-limit rule: no sleeping with them. I snore.

I have the best of both worlds, and the continuous smiles on Mom and Dad's faces are a sure sign of how much I am loved. It sounds like I'm special, and I am.

Excuse me.
It'll only take a few seconds.

Summer and Fall Trails

Freedom Fields County Park

Little Egg Harbor, NJ

Duke

Lots of puppies were visiting the flea market. One day, a lady came to take one of us home, but she didn't stay. My hopes were let down. *Would she ever find me at the boarding house where I lived since I was no longer at the marketplace?* She did locate me, but a man was with her this time. Being macho, I pushed my way to the front of the kennel door for attention. It worked. I got saved from this breeding farm where we slept one on top of each other. Given the name, *Duke* portrayed my character.

My new home was a second-floor apartment over a saloon, where the sounds of music and laughter kept me alert. Finding it hard to sleep, I discovered an overstuffed chair to snuggle up in to drown out the noise. As I outgrew the chair, I traded it in for a full-sized bed to get under the covers.

I loved my mother's high-heeled leather shoes, but she didn't love me for what I did to them. Doing my best to convince her that I was a teething puppy didn't work. Shoes were off-limits.

German Shepherd dogs were known to be big and protective, and within a year, I was no exception. One time, I knocked a man down a flight of steps at the apartment and did my best to blame his fall on him being drunk. Mom scolded me and put a gate at the top of the stairs. That reminded me of the kennel. The only thought that crossed my mind was that I hadn't done my job well enough. I started smiling more often to show my pearly white teeth when there were strangers.

My family moved after building a new home. It was a dream come true to experience lots of freedom. My dad walked me around the farm's boundaries to show me I had a big job to take care of all that land. *Was I up for the task? You betcha!* He put a sign up in the five-hundred-foot driveway. It read: *Beware of Dog. Please blow horn.*

I remembered the day when a man drove his car up the lane, tunneled by twenty-eight pin oaks, and ignored the sign. I was on duty when there was a knock at the door. Screams could be heard a mile away. Mom found the visitor on the roof of his car. Proudly, I did my job and wondered why the guy thought the sign was a joke. Dad took disciplinary action by securing me with a twenty-foot chain. That saddened me, and I sought comfort from my house friend, Tinker Bell, the cat. We often hung out together.

One day, Tinker was missing, and Mom, worried, told me to find her. After frightening that man half to death, I had to redeem myself and return to her good graces. Once again, I needed to prove my "macho" personality. Hours later, I found Tinker in the thick woods and carried her back home in my mouth. Mom's praises filled me joyfully, and my tail couldn't stop wagging.

Tinker hunted for her food and only accepted a bowl of milk from Mom. I was forbidden to drink what belonged to the cat. Sometimes, Tinker didn't want her milk for hours. It was tempting. If no one were home, I'd pace back and forth, watching that untouched bowl of milk. Finally, the ultimate question. *Drink it or leave it?* And, now for the drum roll answer. *What do you think?* I didn't drink Tinker Bell's milk. Tinker Bell trusted me. We had a solid friendship.

I found out I had several personalities: I was protective. I was friendly. I could get depressed. Depressed days were when my mom had to go to town by bus. Being familiar with her routine, she'd lock me in the house alone, forcing me to discover a way to create a disappearing act. Mom's frustration of not finding me meant she'd have to stay home and miss the bus -or- leave without knowing where I was hiding. The bus stop was about a mile down the road.

One day, I thought I'd surprise her. Secretly, I left the house and went to the bus station to wait. Frantic, when she saw me, she tried to send me home. I turned my head nonchalantly and pretended I had no idea who this person was. The bus came, so I got on and found my way to a rear seat. The driver shouted, "Lady, get your dog off the bus!" I weighed 95lbs. She couldn't budge me. I was determined not to be left behind. To make a long story short, Mom missed her bus, and we returned home together. She had to make new plans to trick me when she had to ride the bus next time. However, future tricks have yet to work. Grandmom was called to the rescue for car rides.

I had a particular habit of attempting to blame others for something I did. However, my fart smells were definitely definable. Everyone shouted, "Oh no! Duke, what did you do?" I looked ashamed, but I couldn't help myself. Embarrassed, I'd hide in the laundry room. SURPRISE! THE JOKE WAS REVEALED whenever I did not go to the laundry room. Someone else had to take the blame.

If there was a thunderstorm, I took refuge under the covers of Mom and Dad's bed. I never knew where those sounds and flashing lights came from. Admittedly, that's about the only thing I feared.

With all my personalities and moods, Mom and Dad understood and loved me, and I loved them too.

I lived most of my life on the farm. When I got old, my hip wasn't supporting me anymore. The farm was my haven, and I rested there permanently. *What more could I ask for?*

Holly

I was born during the gift-giving season. when trees were adorned with lights, wreaths of holly hung on doors, and mistletoe to capture the joy of the holidays. *What better time of the year to be adopted? Holly* became the perfect name for me.

Did my parents know I was a unique puppy? My voice doesn't sound like the barks of other dogs. Being a Besenji, I yodel to express my intentions. Sometimes, I sound like I'm yawning or mimicking a word, but I haven't perfected that yet. When I am overly excited, I'm a siren, like a fire station alerting the volunteers. I'm still a puppy.

My dad takes me to the park. Listening to conversations, other dog owners have commented how very distinguished and graceful I am while running. Darting in and out of the trees, my dog friends chase each other like being in a race. We all win. I can tell my dad is proud of me, and my forehead wrinkles to show my understanding of his emotions.

My neighborhood has rabbits that occupy the fields. I love chasing them, but I have yet to catch one.

Often, I'm home alone. Birds intrigue me, and I could sit for long periods just watching what they are doing. They gather twigs and fly away with them, chirp, and sing, sending messages. Since I yodel, I might like to learn to imitate their calls.

My favorite toy is a chew stick, which can fill hours of boredom.

Like a cat, I've I have been known to groom myself. Coming from a central African heritage with many lions, I don't know if others thought I'd behave like a cat.

The one thing I do to get my dad's attention is to nibble on his toes. Otherwise, his ankles are the next best thing if he's wearing shoes. He calls me his one and only daughter. There goes my wrinkled forehead again.

After Mom plays with me, followed by a treat, I get my sweater on for cool nights and hop in bed—it's time to close my eyes.

I still have lots of growing to do. My intelligence and poise will manifest as I mature like other Besenji dogs. There's a lot of potential to enfold. Just give me time. My mom and dad have all the patience needed. They love me.

Rocket

As a male Mini Pincher puppy, small enough to be carefully held in the palm of the worker's hand, I found myself in an emergency animal hospital with no answers about how I got a broken leg. A cast to stabilize my limb limited my walking ability. After two weeks of boarding there, I grew lonely since no one adopted me.

Finally, a couple who owned two dogs and a horse came to my rescue. They frequented the stable where their horse was kept. After a conversation with an attendant, their hearts opened with compassion. They consented to foster me while looking for a permanent home. As I became stronger, I could run on three legs. With the cast still on, I ignored my handicap and quickly darted around the house and the dog park. No longer being called "the dog," I was named *Rocket.*

Various inquiries were made to find me a home, which led to several sleep-overs. I must admit that I deliberately worked against these trials by being unfriendly. My underlying motive was to stay with my foster parents and their two dogs. The horse lived elsewhere in a stable.

When training another one of the dogs in the house to obey directional and polite commands, I observed every instruction. Mom didn't know I was paying attention. I was the one who learned basic commands by watching and included directions to turn right or left and to bow like a gentleman. That gained me "brownie points."

Months and seasons went by, and two years later, I heard my foster dad say, "Maybe we should have named him Boomerang." My perseverance was successful, and I had a permanent home and a *real* mom and dad.

There was a neighbor I liked and enjoyed. Visiting her was safe because I was no longer an orphan. An occasional sleepover at her house suited me fine. It was a place I'd go for dog sitting if Mom or Dad were away for a short time.

While visiting the friendly neighbor, Mom and Dad went shopping one day. It started to rain and thunder, and I became anxious. Somehow, I managed to slip out of the neighbor's door. Hoping to remember the way home, running as fast as I could, I arrived with a sense of security at my doorstep, cold and shivering. Mom and Dad were so startled to see me when they returned! Soaking wet, she picked me up and held me close. Her emotions were mixed: anger and relief at the same time. Dad took things in stride and chalked it up to my determination. I didn't try that excursion again. Whenever it rained, I stayed indoors. I was reluctant to make a social call again for a long time afterward.

Mom baked cupcakes in the kitchen, the non-stop busy place for her neighbor's surprise birthday party. She painstakingly decorated the cupcakes with roses. When out of her sight, my curiosity got the best of me. I wanted to investigate the counter where the irresistible cupcakes that smelled so good were waiting.

Putting on my thinking cap, I jumped onto a nearby sofa, climbed to the back of the furniture, and predicted I'd successfully take one more leap to the countertop.

I landed with a slide right into the tray of cupcakes! With glorious expectation, I licked every sweet cupcake to ensure each tasted alike. Mom had to bake all over again. She was unhappy, but I thought I was clever in meeting my goal. I got into trouble, but afterward, everyone laughed when Mom told the story. She figured out I was smarter than she thought.

Our household started changing. My two dog friends got older and no longer lived with us. Saying goodbye to them was difficult. Becoming the only dog in the house, I got all the attention. Mom and Dad have grown closer to me. I loved that, but I missed my buddies.

Another significant change occurred. Mom was passionate about horses and wanted a ranch with a stable for breeding. We moved to Oregon with six acres of

land. Being raised in a suburban area, the move to the country gave me lots of freedom. No more leashes, confined fences, and chasing squirrels up the tree was living in paradise.

Playing hide-and-seek was fun. Mom dug a hole to plant a tree, and I hid inside it. I could hear her calling, "Rocket, Rocket, where are you?"[1]

---

[1] (Author's note: You cannot see Rocket; he's playing hide-and-seek in the deep hole.)

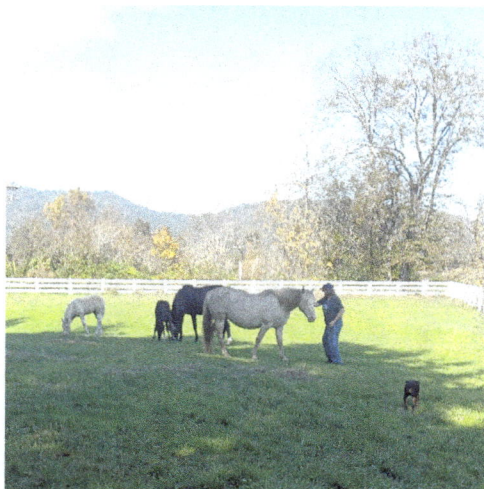

We now have three horses that live in the stable next to our house. I was always terrified of their sizes. *Being 11 lbs., can you imagine standing next to those giants?*

One day, Mom tricked me. She wanted a picture of me and one of her horses. I nipped his nose as she held me in her arms to be nearer the horse. Despite no retaliation from this giant, I remained distant and didn't change my defensive attitude.

Another bonus is frequent car rides for errands. Anywhere I'd go, my ears perked with enthusiasm. Sitting on the car armrest beside Dad allowed me to view everything outside, including vehicles passing close to us. People waved and smiled. I tried not to be distracted so I could keep my eyes on the road.

Sometimes, I sing for my supper by barking for chicken. I'm the chicken boss in the house. Nothing tastes better than a good chicken dinner. It doesn't need to have gravy on it. I don't eat cupcakes anymore.

Becoming a country dog sure did beat neighborhood living. The fresh air and all that space soothed my heart and soul.

I love sitting on Dad's lap at the end of the day, but cuddling between Mom and Dad in bed is heaven. They can feel my stumpy tail wag, revealing my bond and love for them. They give me a goodnight kiss, and all is right in my world, except for the horses.

Welcoming Spring

Maggie

In a wooded country area of South Jersey, a privately owned breeder with a litter of yellow labs was looking to find homes for these heart-warming puppies. Residents and friends were excited to bring a puppy home to love.

At ten weeks old, I was adopted by a single man who wanted a dog to be his best friend. Several names were tossed up, and the perfect name of Maggie was spoken in his soft voice.

My new dad gave me lots of attention, and being satisfactorily trained to his expectations, I started going on job sites with him. His truck carried lots of plumbing tools and supplies, and with limited space, I was assigned the passenger seat next to him.

Upon returning home after Dad's exhausting day, I'd coax him to throw a Frisbee until it was my turn to be exhausted, and then relaxation time followed. Dad would lay on the sofa and close his eyes, and I did the same on my *"rug"* (the name for my large, firm dog bed). Soft stuffed animals kept me company.

Not wholly grown up yet, a big dog growled at me while Dad and I were hanging out at the marina where his boat was docked. I'm sure my size didn't threaten him. *Was he being territorial? Was he being a bully?* After that incident, my decision to socialize with other dogs wasn't a priority. I preferred the company of people.

As years went by, I was still a working dog. There was no one like Dad. He had become my best friend UNTIL ONE DAY . . .

Who was this? Dad had a girlfriend. As I watched them hug and kiss, I'd bark to show my jealousy, letting them know *this was my house and he belonged to me.*

It took some time to get used to having her around, and it prompted me to become more friendly with the two cats by permitting them to cuddle with me on my *rug.* I thought that would make Dad and his girlfriend jealous, but it didn't work. They got married.

My new mom did everything she could to win me over, and it worked. Becoming her kitchen assistant, I gratefully accepted home-cooked meals and offered myself as a permanent dishwasher.

Mom and Dad had their way of talking to me, a language no other dogs understood.

My bags, including my dish, were packed when preparing for vacation. That confirmed without hesitation that I was going. My adrenaline surged with the words, *"OOOH! Big day tomorrow,"* but not all car rides were getaways.

The nearby park had wooded trails hidden from the parking areas. This park was a haven for lots of dogs. However, there were restrictions. I complied with the sign "Dogs must be on a leash." I carried the leash in my mouth, but the park guards must have been spying on me, hiding behind big trees. I got into trouble, and Mom was given an off-leash warning, not just once, but several times. Being attached to a leash was punishment enough, despite the citation she eventually received for disobeying the leash rules.

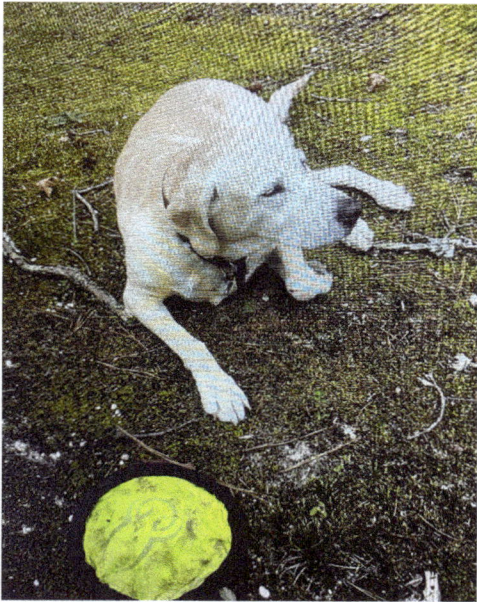

Car rides to run errands with Mom replaced working with Dad in his plumbing business. "Do you want to go in the Cadillac?" Even though I had dirty paws because I had an affinity for playing in puddles, the old run-down car didn't need extra protection to stay clean. It was the perfect car for me.

Playing with my "*pocketbook*" became a family affair. Mom and Dad tossed the Frisbee back and forth to each other. My job was to intercept the pass as I leaped three feet in the air, sailing like a gazelle, to complete a dynamic catch. With cheers of excitement, "*Bonus!*" meant I did a great job and got ready for another round. The Frisbee was round, soft, and comfortable to carry in my mouth, and it looked like a pocketbook.

These secret words developed were our unique code. However, when it was my turn to speak to reveal what was on my mind if my wishes were unmet, I'd hear Mom or Dad call out, "State your case." My challenge was to bark specifically for what I wanted: a treat, a walk, a Frisbee, or kitchen duty. Barks could be soft, several barks in a row; barks with a dance or two, giving my paw to reach out for acknowledgment; and loud, strong barks meant guard dog alert.

After practicing my barking methods of communication, I perfected a sound when opening my mouth to yawn, repeating that motion several times, and blurted out, *Wa, wa, yew?* (Translated into: Where were you?) It was my way of letting them know I didn't like being home alone. Mom and Dad were amazed at how I spoke.

It took some time for her to become my second-best friend, but when Dad was home, I reluctantly admitted that she was "chopped liver." She may have ruled the house when he was working, but being Dad's "sweetheart," I could do no wrong and was referred to as "Queen Sheba."

After sixteen years, getting old slowed me down. Losing my hearing and having diminishing eyesight, Mom became my full-time caregiver and met all my needs, including daily fresh bedding. I realized I had two best friends.

After I permanently retired, a portrait of me hangs in their living room. Everyone who sees it reminisces about the mutual love and gratitude that permeated our home. That's an unforgettable legacy.

Maggie

Oso

Being a seven-pound male Chihuahua mix, I grew up along the northern Mexican border, where the desert begged for rain.

I lived with a man whose stature overpowered me. To keep out the sun, he covered his head with a sombrero. Wearing big boots, I skirted around his gait and often got in the way. *Did he kick me on purpose?* After that incident, I decided I liked women more than men. That created a personality conflict. Being tagged as unmanageable, I was forfeited to a home for fearful Chihuahuas. Of course, that misinterpreted my personality; I wasn't fearful but opinionated and was unlikeable to this hombre.

After my initial stay in a Mexican rescue center, I was relocated to a Humane Society in Southern California and given the name *Oso*, a shortened version of *Osito* (little bear). *Why the name Osito?* It was the next letter in the alphabet for naming rescue dogs. My true character was covered up by being photogenic. I was adopted immediately with no mention of being fearful or unmanageable.

Surprise! After adoption, my hyperactive conduct surfaced. Everything spooked me in a residential neighborhood. Attacking and growling at big or small dogs could have resulted in unfavorable consequences, but I was naive.

Unacceptable conduct dictated a new direction. Mom enrolled me with a behaviorist trainer who was persistent in helping me adapt. Sessions lasted for eighteen months. How to accept other dogs was puzzling. The trainer attached a leash to various stuffed dogs of different sizes and pretended she was walking them. Homework with mom led to a voice command of 'YIP", followed by a treat. That helped me to discover that other dogs could be gentle.

Success happened. I had terrific improvement and could walk with five other dogs in my neighborhood as if in a parade. The pack tempered other strange dogs, which helped me tone down any underlying aggression.

On individual outings, Mom loved to stop and smell the flowers, and following in her footsteps, I also delighted in the intoxicating aroma. Flowers brought out my mellow side, and their fragrance has become essential to our walks.

Wearing a red sweater, gifted by Mom, comforts me. It's the security of her continued presence when she's working. The astroturf in my backyard can be super-heated from the sun, a reminder of the hot temperatures in Mexico, but I still wanted my sweater on.

When Mom returns from work, the first thing she does is hold me in her arms like a burping baby. Grasping with my four paws, I manage to hug her back. Happily sitting together in her recliner, savoring the moment, our breathing synchronizes, and my muscles go limp. With a relaxing sigh, *I know Mom's home.*

My expected daily kibble meals are topped with shredded cheese, green beans, and chopped chicken pieces to vary my menu. Fresh strawberries, peaches, and watermelon satisfy my thirst on hot days.

My first choice is a machaca burrito, retaining a Mexican tradition. Mom can't fool me when she makes anything with scrambled eggs. I'll wait for a handout.

Throwing toys in the air fires up my vitality. Stuffed animals have lost their eyes and ears due to my enthusiastic activities. My toys have names: *Bozo* looks like a bear; *Squirrel* is just called squirrel, a gift from my grandma; and *Ducky* squeaks and is small enough to carry in my mouth, which was given to me by my trainer. Hidden are five reserved stuffed toys, but Mom doesn't know that I know about them.

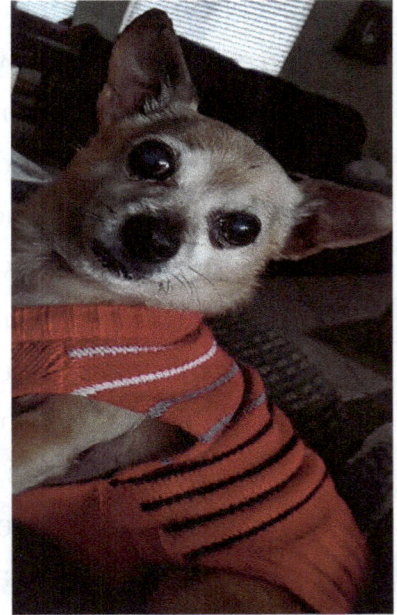

There's a restricted room with a three-foot-high doorway gate to slow down my energy. When rested enough, and with my perfected jumping skills, I spring like a bouncing ball over the gate, and I'm ready to play again.

Life isn't perfect, but it's close. I have been taken to the vet yet to pinpoint the reason for my chronic skin irritation. Since I suffer from unbearable itching, I take medications to control blisters and open sores. As Mom sings, "A spoonful of sugar helps the medicine go down- - - (la la la)- - - in a most delightful way."[1] (Quietly thinking: *It must be good for me because she's smiling while singing.*)

The tablets are buffered with cream cheese or peanut butter. The liquid meds are hidden in powdered peanut butter with water added. I do my best to spit the dosages out of my mouth, but with coverups and Mom's singing, I tolerate the horrible taste.

I do love bathing twice a week. That soothes my skin. I wear an after-shower robe until I completely dry off, which substitutes for my much-loved sweater.

On days when Mom works at home, I'm her computer assistant. I hold her left arm with my paw while she types with one right-hand finger, supervising for typos. Even with my help, she could be a better typist.

My active lifestyle hasn't completely changed, but I've transformed how I handle daily ups and downs. Mom is alpha; I'm part of a pack of dogs. Her love and acceptance persevered with my initial behaviors.

---

[1] "A Spoon for of Sugar" is a song from "Mary Poppins." A 1964 Walt Disney musical motion picture.

I'm here to stay. At night, I sleep in a crate that looks like an igloo. I don't want to disturb Mom when I itch at night. She understands me, and in the morning, after a night's sleep – our love continues.

Rusty

One day, I woke up at a shelter called "Mama's-gona Rescue."[2] *I am still determining how I got there.* Along with other dogs, we were all transported in crates to a country store and put on display for sale or adoption. I am a six-pound Maltipoo with brown curly hair. That was why I was named *Rusty*. I noticed an elderly lady staring at me. With my big brown eyes, I flirted with her, hoping she'd swoop me up and cuddle me. Sadly, seeing her leave, I kept my paws crossed that she'd return.

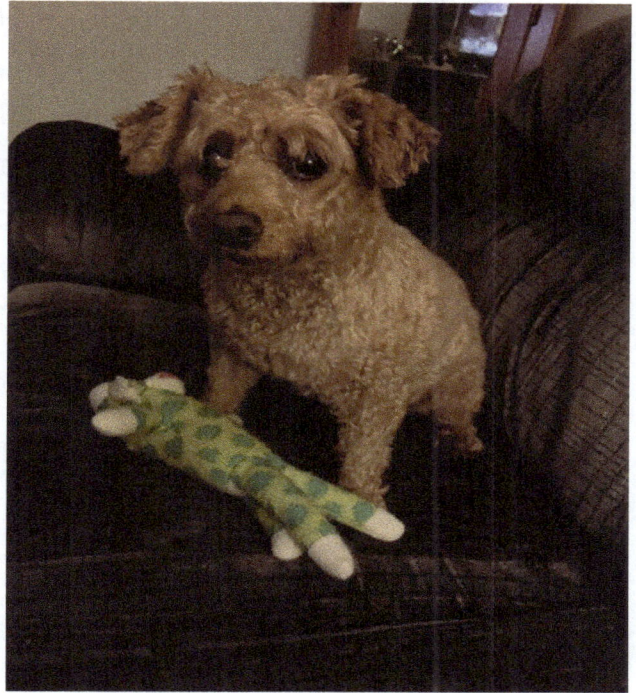

I slept that night dreaming of her as my new rescue mama. The dream became a reality when this lovely lady came back for me the following day. Excited about a new home, I hoped I didn't disappoint her when she discovered I wasn't housebroken. I tried to be good. She understood this dilemma, and shortly afterward, I got into an acceptable routine. Her patience was a virtue.

---

[2] "Mama's-gona Rescue." 501(c)(3) Rescue Group., Egg Harbor City, NJ

Eating chocolate brownies from the coffee table got me into trouble. Learning a hard lesson, I became sick with an upset stomach. No more stealing food without permission. Mom and I had a serious talk about my eating habits.

With her understanding ways, we started sharing meals together. What delightful menus! Sometimes chicken. Sometimes beef. Sometimes lamb. *Was I being rewarded for making a mistake about the dessert I made disappear?* Delighted in home cooking and the goodies she gave me; the maximum she wanted me to weigh was fifteen pounds. Snacks became limited. My personality could be demanding when I barked for water and flip my dish when it's empty. Water was safe, no extra calories.

Park walks were where I found a buddy named Benji. One day, I was walking through the trails with Mom when my ears perked up. I heard Benji's bark and knew he was calling for me. I sprung loose from my leash and made a hundred-yard dash through the thick woods to search for my best friend. Darting here and there, we found each other happy as a lark. Our simultaneous barks were the only way my mom and Benji's Dad found us.

After that, we decided on a meeting place by one of the park benches. Seasons came and went. We had frequent play dates until something changed. Benji didn't come to play. Sadly, I learned about dog heaven.

Mom started taking me to another park with a lake. The sunsets were beautiful, a romantic paradise. It embarrassed Mom when I got into a habit of curiously watching strangers. Others thought Mom was doing the staring, but it was me. That prompted us to stop, chat, and make new friends. I overheard people say, "He looks like a stuffed toy teddy bear." So, I was the one who was getting all the attention, not Mom.

I found a tiny herring in a shallow puddle of water at the lake park. I hope I didn't scare the little flopping fish when I growled. I am still determining how he got there, but I wondered if a boy carrying a bucket of water had live bait.

Days weren't always perfect. I encountered three unfriendly German Shepherds. They entered my backyard uninvited and attacked me. What a fearful experience. I went to the vet's office for immediate first aid to treat the lacerations. After getting bandaged up, I was so glad to be back home. I wouldn't say I liked the slurpy liquid medication. Mom tried to hide the pills in some cheese. Somehow, I couldn't fool her by spitting everything out when she wasn't watching. That was unacceptable, and I should have known better since Mom was a nurse.

After that episode, big dogs or anything oversized made me more fearful and alert. My walks became extra cautious. One day, I noticed something trailing behind me, and without hesitation, I growled and became defensive. *Was I protecting myself or Mom's welfare, or was I just scared?* With a sigh of relief, she explained it was an air-filled goblin, a Halloween decoration caught in the wind.

The mail truck was one of my highlights of living in the country with a few neighbors. One day, a fruit arrangement came for Mom, and I kept my hopes up that I might get something special. *Would I ever get anything? Maybe from Chewy. com?* [1] My expectations were granted, and now I get a dog treat from the mail lady each time Mom receives a package. Those occasional calorie snacks don't count.

Everyday walks and sitting on a park bench watching the world go by add to my joy. I don't prefer car rides - I'm the outdoor type. When I'm not ready to go home, I sit like a statute, and Mom has to pick me up and carry me to the car. I'm probably spoiled, but I won't let her know.

I lead a simple life: good food and friends; I enjoy cuddling next to Mom when she watches TV, reads a book, or does needlepoint. She permits me to get comfortable on the sofa. Furniture naps are not off-limits. What else do I need?

I look forward to regular bedtime hours. *Am I part of a royal household sharing Mom's King-sized bed?* It's time for sweet dreams as I nestle with my pillow and blanket. I do believe that dreams can come true. It did for me.

---

[1] Chewy.com Online supplier of pet foods and supplies.

Sammy
(California)

Living in a military base animal shelter wasn't easy. I was anxious and scared. Loud noises from helicopters, tanks, and other activities didn't resonate with me as a puppy. I was separated from my mama dog, and the sleeping quarters weren't cozy. Several marine families wanted to adopt me. However, repeated delays in a pick-up date created a sign-up waitlist. *I must have been popular.*

A couple often came to see me, who was second on the long list. As promised to the first soldier, the calendar days went by slowly. *Would the two-week wait ever happen?* The day finally arrived. The big clock on the wall was near closing time, and my inner anxiety was building.

The first listed person has yet to show up. The alternate couple that visited me frequently had their fingers crossed in anticipation of adopting me. At five o'clock sharp, the uniformed guard, who stood with full attention, pointed at the couple and declared with a firm voice, "A marine is never late. The dog is yours." My new dad was saluted with respect. I discovered he was a retired Navy Master Chief and immediately wondered if I would live in a house with strict rules. I shook while riding in the car, sitting on my new mom's lap.

The government is often referred to as "Uncle Sam." With a military background, I was given the name *Sammy*.

Wondering what kind of mixed-breed dog I was, the question was settled: *"Sammy, the wonder dog. We wonder what he is."* I may have been a cockapoo, but I'm not sure. I had ears like a spaniel. I overheard Dad say, "He's going to shed a lot." Generally, poodles don't shed. Mom already fell in love with me and didn't care if I shed. *What a relief!*

Being insecure, they bought me a knotted rope that I carried in my mouth. My pacifier was named "rope-a-dope." When asked where it was, I'd hunt the house until I found it. *I loved my "rope-a-dope."*

I was still a young puppy when the vet diagnosed me with a severe throat problem that caused me to vomit after meals. My eating dish was elevated to make swallowing easier. Mom, being a chiropractor, gave me special hands-on attention, and it helped me to eat and feel better. Signs that meant HELP included choking, falling, vomiting, and dizziness. She understood and responded quickly. This challenge was lifelong, but I was happy with my mom taking care of me.

Even though Dad and I were bonded, when I displayed the HELP signs, and Mom was out of town, my care was limited to phone calls. He'd say, *"Console your son."* Her voice was a comfort. Dad understood and took my needs seriously. Like me, he had health challenges with frequent visits to the hospital. During those times, while he was away if I could smell his clothes, I knew he was OK.

I tried to convince Mom to take me on her out-of-town educational seminars. I'd bring my rope to her suitcase and give her an innocent stare. Sometimes it worked, and sometimes it didn't. I feared not having Mom near me if I got sick again.

To make life a little easier, Mom took me to her office. The office manager didn't like dogs. Visits became limited to days when no patients were scheduled. A sign in the window saying "Sammy is here" alerted the UPS lady to make an unofficial stop to play with me. It was a highlight.

I was excited when Mom closed her full-time practice and opened a part-time home office. Not only did I need additional care because I developed seizures, but Dad also needed more attention and care.

Frequent vet visits and my mom's chiropractic treatment became a routine in maintaining my health. I'd jump up on the adjusting table for immediate attention if a seizure were approaching. HELP signs allowed me to communicate. Sometimes, the seizures would abort, and sometimes, they were minimal with her care. Mom knew what to do.

Being with her daily as she treated patients, I became a therapy dog. Calling out, "Find your rope-a-dope," gave patients joy when I returned to the office carrying it in my mouth. They'd tell me I was a role model for being such a happy dog despite poor health.

Dad thought it was time to have quality vacations as a family, so we started RVing. It was essential for us to be together. Dad was admitted to the hospital after one of our RV trips. He was concerned not only for his health but for mine as well.

Sudden changes took place. My well-being declined. I lost my balance and hearing, all at the same time, while Dad was critically struggling for life in the hospital. Mom was overwhelmed. Her tears fell onto my face. As she held me in her arms, the phone rang. Dad called to see how I was. I could sense his faint voice, and with Mom holding me so closely, I slipped away while they told me how much I was loved.

I may have had many health challenges, but I was a happy dog. For 14 years, I was indeed their "wonder dog." It's incredible how my life unfolded. My parents loved me with compassion, acceptance, and understanding. Mom often sang to me. I worked as a therapy dog, went on exciting vacations, and slept between my mom and dad at night. Providence led me to the perfect family. That was my life and my message.

Oscar

After a long truck ride from Arkansas to Toms River, New Jersey, I arrived with my brothers and sisters to be housed in a charitable rescue facility. While there, I was given the name *Spike*, probably because I have a long white streak on my face, which starts on my forehead and ends at my nose. Lots of people visited, looking to take one of us home.

My eyes met with a lady who fetched me up into her arms. As I experienced her warmth, we fell in love. She whispered to me, "You are my Oscar." *Did she get me mixed up with one of my brothers since we looked much alike? Was my fairy tale of instant love going to end because she called me Oscar, not Spike?* With a deep, soft, heartfelt voice, she told me she found a dog named Oscar on the internet with an expectation of adoption. Fortunately for me, someone else claimed him. With a sigh of relief, this gentle lady was mine. I demonstrated my joy with powerful leaps straight up in the air and simultaneously threw kisses.

My new mom started taking me on playdates to meet other dogs. Being so enthusiastic, not all dogs understood that I only wanted to play. A fighter, I am not. Any confrontation would **not** have originated in my mind, even though other dogs may be on the defensive with pit bulls. That's seventy-five percent of my heritage.

One time, when I carried a stick in my mouth, another dog wanted to grab it from me. That was selfish. When trying to take that stick away from me, I got bit. and my ear bled; I cried as I fell to the ground. Remorse from the other dog was apparent as my playmate hid under a tree for a long time. Forgiving him, we became friends again.

Here's a big question. *Why is this?* Females like me and often are looking for my attention. There is a gentleman-like appearance about me. My coat is brown, and I have a white chest, which looks like I'm wearing a tailored suit. I am still determining from which side of my family I inherited my good looks. *Or, is it the shampoo Mom uses to bathe me that has an irresistible scent that attracts?* In any event, I have to put my foot down by grumbling at these ladies: *Not today.* Sometimes they understand, and sometimes they don't. But, being a gentleman, I thank my lucky stars for running off-leash and playing with no strings attached.

However, there was a time when I liked being trapped by two Newfoundlands squeezing between them. They each weighed about 160 lbs. I weigh 78 lbs. I'm like a peanut butter and marshmallow sandwich. They liked me, and I like them, so it's acceptable.

Every day, Mom drives me to the park in her pick-up truck. That's our routine. When she surprises me with shopping trips to Tractor Supply[1] and Pet Smart[2], I cry excitedly!

Home life is excellent. I'm a watchdog and lie in our front yard to watch everything and everyone. If someone approached, I'd tell my mom someone was there, but I'd wag my tail and welcome them. So… maybe I'm not the definition of a watchdog. *Am I supposed to growl and bark impolitely?*

Being like an energizer bunny, I keep going and going and am ready for any activity that comes my way. That works up an appetite at the end of the day, followed by a cookie for dessert.

I eventually inherited my bedroom and bed when my mom's son grew up and moved out of the house. What a privilege to have my own space.

I enjoy life. I know I taught my mom to enjoy her life more each day. Our love at first sight grew and grew. She's my best friend and tells me I'm her best friend too. Thanks, Mom.

In Memorium
Oscar unexpectedly crossed over the bridge before the publication of this book.
The dog owner chose not to alter his story. Thank you. Oscar is missed.

---

[1] Tractor Supply C° serves recreational farmers, ranchers, homeowners, gardeners, and pet enthusiasts.
[2] Pet Smart is an American-owned superstore chain for pet supplies and services.

Ollie

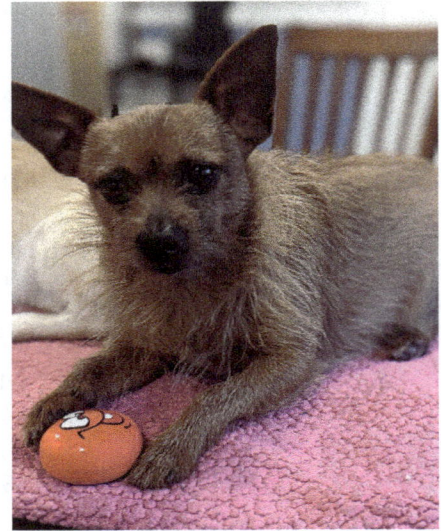

Appearing on Facebook with my brothers and sisters, we had no idea how we arrived at a foster home. It was a place where we joined other dogs and patiently waited to find a forever home.

Somehow, I managed to nestle my way onto a young girl's lap for hugs and kisses, winning the affection of a lady and her daughter. Being a Chorkie (mixed breed Chihuahua and Yorkshire Terrier), I innately knew I'd be loyal. Given that the name *Oliver* was too formal, but I accepted it. After a while, I was called *"Ollie."* That suited me better.

A big day happened when I was enrolled in dog training classes to learn basic commands. I thought I was the perfect dog, but my mom thought I needed formal education. Being a sweet dog, I complied because I didn't want to disappoint her. Recognizing that the other dogs in the program had learning challenges, I was proud of myself because I picked up directions or instructions fast.

It wasn't long before I grew up to be a charming young dog and fell in love with a Pomeranian. I became the proud daddy of three puppies, who were as cute as a button. Sadly, their mother rejected them. *What's a dad to do? Did I have any motherly instincts?* The babies had to be bottle-fed, while I took up the role of cuddling them to reassure them that Daddy loved them. My protective eye allowed them to roam and play, and as they got older, I visualized they'd soon have a place of their own.

One puppy chose to stay with me. The other siblings were adopted and relocated to a home nearby, where I visited them for oodles of play dates. With twinkles in their eyes, they watched out the window as they waited for me to arrive. A sure hint that they enjoyed life.

Who was this elderly lady, called Grandma, that visited often? Family ties had grown, and I bonded with her more and more. Frequent stopovers had been to check up on her daughter, but somehow, I got all the attention. Grandma had a scent that I couldn't identify. *Was it perfume? Shampoo?* Whatever it was, I would meet her nose-to-nose.

Soon after, I was called "Ollie, the hero dog." With my keen sense of smell and after several nose-to-nose contacts, Grandma's scent revealed a basal cell carcinoma. After a medical doctor confirmed my findings, she continued to have regular second opinions from me. She told me our follow-ups had been of great importance to her.

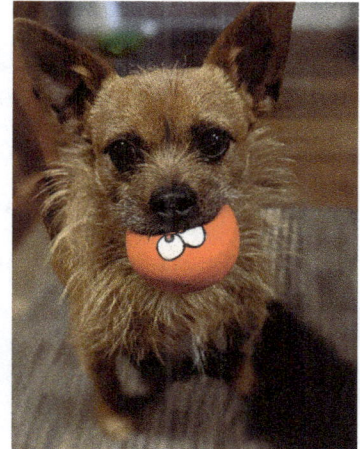

Being young, I loved squeaky toys and played with them for hours. My favorite red ball with a face on it has been like a friend with a continuous smile. I did my best to persuade Mom to throw my ball back and forth, but the repetition tired her, and she begged me to slow down.

To burn off my unlimited energy, I run along the neighbor's fence, where a German Shepherd willingly accompanies me. There's no comparison of my weight of ten pounds to his muscular structure of seventy pounds; I have also managed to tire him out.

In our house, we have four cats. Allowing three of them to invade my territory is OK, but it's off-limits for one cat because she scratched my eye, and it hurt. Another thing about the naughty cat: she has attempted to steal my favorite liverwurst treat. By the way, even though I look like a Taco Bell dog, I still haven't acquired a taste for Mexican food. To make a long story short, I had to set boundaries for the cat, which had no manners, but the other three cats were my buddies.

Dress me up in the winter? No thanks. Why? Mom thinks I need a covering because other dogs have sweaters, jackets, and rain gear. All that stuff gets in the way of my energetic nature. I'd rather just "rough it" in the cold weather.

Days are complete, and when Mom says, "Nite, nite," I welcome bedtime. After she kisses me and tells me I'm her sweetheart, we cuddle together for a good night's sleep. When morning arrives, I patiently wait for her to open her eyes before we start a new day. This beats foster home living. Thanks!

Tugger

There was a story and an appeal in a local newspaper. ***Dog hit by a car. Homes needed for orphans.*** Having several siblings, neighborhood residents responded, and an empathetic couple adopted me.

That same newspaper had another story. It was 1980 when the Phillies won the World Series, a great event for Pennsylvania fans. The winning pitcher was Tug McGraw, and baseball enthusiasts celebrated. I was named *Tugger*.

Living up to my name. I became obsessed with ball playing. Practicing around the clock, I chose a tennis ball rather than a hard ball. Tennis balls bounced, hard balls didn't.

The other team members were my mom and dad. Bringing them the ball and playing catch was serious business. My goal was to master fly balls as well as grounders. When they needed time-outs, I discovered I could dart up to the top of the staircase with a ball in my mouth, and the next maneuver was to push the ball down with my nose. I challenged myself to catch the ball before it landed at the bottom of the steps. There were many errors at first, but I demonstrated perfection with practice. I wasn't a pitcher like McGraw, but I could've been a valuable player on any team.

It puzzled me to discover a new kind of ball suspended from a tree. Instead of bouncing, it burst sharply in my mouth. Mom explained that they were Christmas ornaments and the lights weren't treats.

Packages from Santa Claus were fun for me to chew up. Once again, Mom had to tell me that not all gifts were meant for Tugger. Since Christmas was my favorite holiday, I had to apply self-control year after year.

One summer, vacationing in the Pocono Mountains of Pennsylvania, our campsite was by a lake. I couldn't resist diving into the water to cool off from the heat. Catching a fish, it wiggled and wiggled in my mouth. As I brought it to the shore, Mom and Dad laughed. *What was wiggling faster, the fish or my tail?* Vacations were a highlight. Freedom.

Home life was only sometimes at home. When Mom and Dad couldn't find me, they realized I snuck out for visits to see my girlfriends. Being attracted to females, I became a dad several times.

When I returned from one of my excursions, happy as a lark, Mom wondered what I was chewing and why I stood crooked. Lo and behold, she wasn't overly pleased about my delightful find. Discovering marijuana under a bush in the neighborhood, I ate it. It was like trying a new menu at a restaurant with apparent results.

There were many activities, with and without my family. Freedom was a choice they offered me, and they knew I'd always return. Their understanding and love gave me a perfect home. Being a "mutt" meant *I was a special mutt since I was named after a celebrity.* I wondered if my other mutt brothers and sisters had a good life like I did. I hoped so.

I retired at sixteen and met my Dad, who had already crossed over the bridge. Welcome home.

Bleu

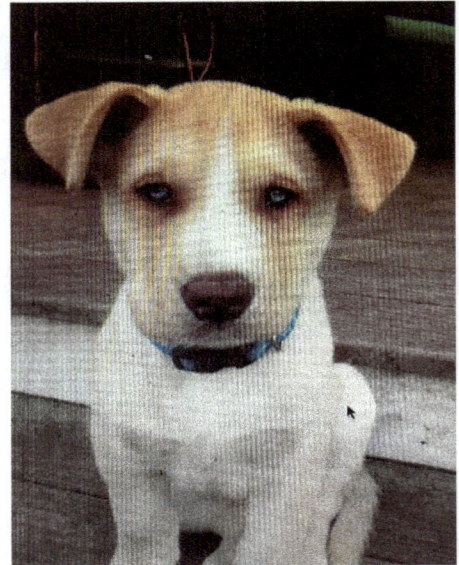

I was one of nine puppies from a surprise litter. Word got out, and several families stepped up to the plate. We all needed a home, so our pictures were circulated. *Would I be one of the lucky ones?*

My *almost* new mom had to persuade her husband that a dog would be welcome. He wasn't keen on the idea and insisted on not seeing any puppy pictures. After a glass of wine, she swayed her mellow-hearted husband into adopting me. With captivating blue eyes, I secured a home. That's how I got the name *Bleu.*

Shortly after my adoption, a few sharing friends posted me on an Instagram page. While attending a local festival, I was recognized. "Are you Bleu?" Mom was puzzled about how her new beloved Bleu had turned into a celebrity. Teenagers had spread the word.

An art school student painted a portrait of me. Ironically, it became a Father's Day gift to the Dad I once had to convince.

Being a husky/lab, born to be a runner, no one could catch me; therefore, my ambitions were restricted. On leashed walks, I developed an intense curiosity for active building sites. Construction workers hypnotized me with their projects. I'd

146

request permission to investigate with my keen sense of smell to get closer to the activities. My mom tells me she was convinced I had a previous life in that line of work. *Is that possible?*

Park visits, a highlight of my day, satisfied my freedom to run and play with other dogs, but one time, the car ride wasn't to the park. It was long, and I had yet to learn where I was going. After several days, the destination was somewhere other than home. It was exciting, but I was also worried. *Where was I? Did I move? Will I ever see my friends again at the dog park?*

The journey ended in a remote place in Florida. The nature preserves had only a handful of people around and a few houses.

This new environment captured my curiosity for water. All kinds of water: ponds, lakes, bogs, and moving water as far as I could see. My attraction led me to a marsh where I could view and fantasize about what was on the other side. *Are there things I could play with, eat, or hide?* Ideas were endless. Since I didn't like swimming, I decided I'd keep chasing turtles back into the grassy bogs within my reach.

Watching Mom water ski fascinated me until, one time, she disappeared. As fear distressed me, I jumped off the dock to save her, but instead, she rescued me. I found out that swimming definitely was not my cup of tea. I didn't do that again, but watching that water sport afterward provided entertainment.

Several long round-trip rides continued for four years. Growing accustomed to New Jersey and Florida homes made me wonder if everything would be the same when I returned to each location.

Something did change—no vacation for one year. We stayed in New Jersey. My mother's sister needed my attention and love, and I never hesitated to be with her until she left us. This overwhelming sadness happened on my mom's birthday.

Shortly after that, thoughts surfaced about becoming a therapy dog. The COVID pandemic changed the course of events. No certified training classes were available. That was OK. The ability to comfort was naturally built into me. My wagging tail tells the story of when the emotions of others go up or down.

The announcement came again. Off to Florida. Another long ride. Stopping off at campgrounds, exploring the trails, watching squirrels climb trees, birds eating cubes of bread from campers, and so many happy children. At night, when it was dark, fire pits near our tent invited me not to roam. It was cozy, and I loved camping.

Once again, while in Florida, thinking I had overcome my aversion to water, I decided that a shallow pond was OK. But - *Oh no! It wasn't*. It turned out to be a swamp, consuming me very quickly. I barked for help continuously while my Dad and neighbors scouted for me.

Fearing alligators, snakes, and snapping turtles that occupied the swamp, my Dad was in harm's way. With a rope tied around him, his bravery saved me.

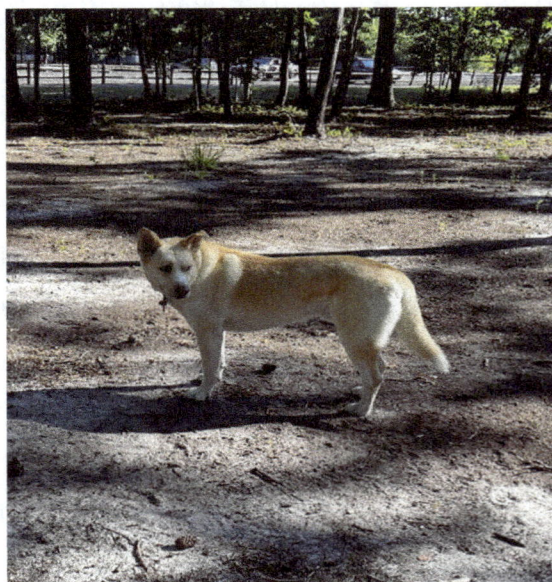

Neighbors pulled us both out of this threatening place. *What a way to show their love on Valentine's Day.*

I didn't want newspaper reporters and begged Dad to keep this event a secret. I learned my lesson again. Wandering out of the fenced yard was taboo.

Water, water. I certainly had several water experiences. However, what comes out of the water *does* appeal to me. I love salmon. Fish dinners keep my yellow coat smooth and shiny.

My internal clock tells me that 9 p.m. is bedtime. Sometimes, I wish my mom and dad knew how to tell time. I like sleeping with them, so I patiently wait for them to join me.

Being a blue-eyed husky bred to be a sled-pulling dog, I have dreams of what snow might be like. *Maybe someday Mom and Dad might surprise me with a cold wintry trip.*

Life is good, except for being in the water. I've grown to love all the adventures. Thanks to them, I joined the perfect family for fun and excitement.

Brutus

It puzzled me why I ended up in a shelter. *Was it because I peed in the house when I wasn't supposed to?* But that's how I claimed my territory. Having a lot to say, I yapped often. *Could that be another reason?*

No one told me how I got the name *Brutus* since I was a hand-me-down.

One day, a tall man with a white beard, like mine, visited the shelter, searching for the right companion to take home. Relating to him immediately, with excitement, I peed on his shoe, and that's all it took. We claimed each other.

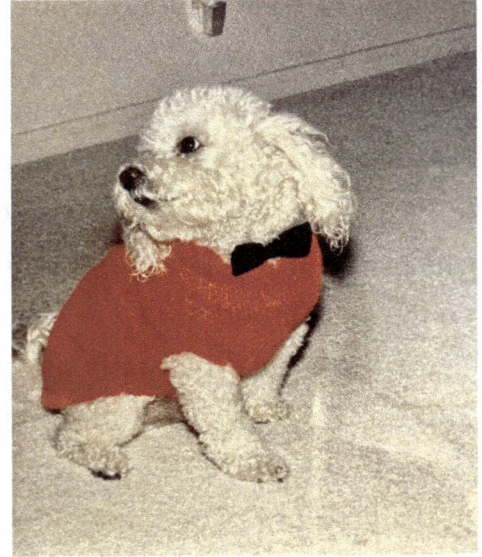

It was time to meet this man's wife, and I was warned that she liked big dogs and was introduced to her huge stuffed animal friend. I knew we'd get along since there was no response to my barking. Being a handsome eleven-pound fluffy Bichon, I was confident I could win her. Swooping me up into her arms, I could tell she liked me. I didn't pee on her.

My new parents accepted my frequent barking; it was music to their ears. They wanted a friendly dog, and I was perfect for them. Eventually, I greeted Mom with my version of "*maw, maw,*" just like any other child, happy to see their mom.

As she brought out the best of me, I tried not to pee in the house. However, accidents did happen. *Why do I have that frequent habit? I'm still working on figuring that out.*

Being a thriving California dog, I lived in a townhouse near the beach. During frequent walks to the State Park, I saw dogs of all sizes having fun in RVs. My new parents also had an RV, and I was excited to know I'd join them on vacation.

In our travels, we walked through an old mining town in Jerome, Arizona. It was the perfect area to make a pit stop because the building signs read "MEN" and "WOMEN." Mom and Dad laughed when I heard them say, "I think Brutus can read. Maybe he'll get the message."

While in Louisiana, seeing insects, critters, and all that roamed the earth was new to me. With so many buggy areas, I scratched a lot. Baths were not my favorite, and I was not too fond of the hose being squirted on me, but it felt good afterward.

When we visited Niagara Falls, I kept my paws crossed that I wouldn't be in one of those baths. Declining politely, I backed away and pretended the falls didn't frighten me. Happily, I remained in the RV and waited patiently for their return.

Seeing the deep snow and hopping around in it for the first time was fun. The cold drifts came up to my neck. Being white on white, I could disappear like a magician. The Colorado mountains were the last stop on this magnificent journey. However, I looked forward to returning to sunny Southern California.

The smells were great on this trip, far surpassing my backyard's minimal sniffs. What a lucky dog! The trip was sixteen thousand miles, and it took several months. However, there was no place like home, and I immediately took possession of my surroundings.

Familiar with the front doorbell alert, I made my barking announcement every time I heard it. *Who was visiting? Why was no one there?* My parents laughed when there was a commercial on TV with the same doorbell ring. I never did figure that out.

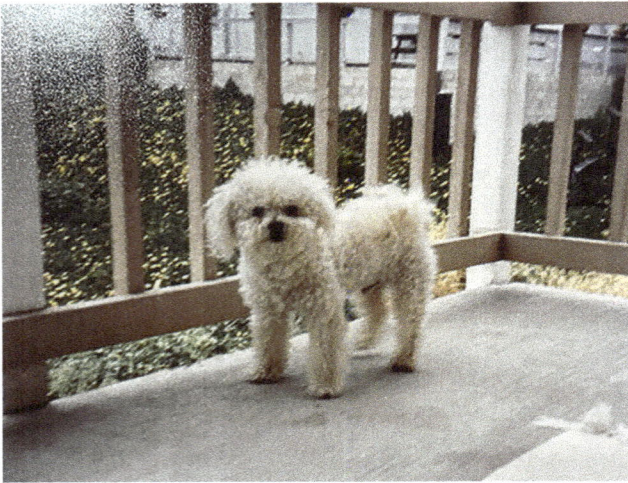

When my uncle visited, he didn't use the front door. He drove up in his loud, rumbling motorcycle. Peeking out the balcony railings of our townhouse, I yapped with excitement!

One day, I heard the motorcycle sound and greeted my uncle, but he didn't respond. I got concerned and couldn't understand why I was being avoided. Finally, Mom took me to where the motorcycle was parked. It wasn't my uncle but a police officer doing a neighborhood watch. The cop didn't hesitate to tell me I was "blowing his cover" because I wouldn't shut up. I was tricked.

News was delivered that my uncle was getting married. *What would that mean? Would I be included in the wedding?* The day came, and I proudly wore a black bow tie and stood next to the Best Man. I was the "Best Dog."

I was included in all family affairs, including quiet times. Mom liked to play a CD while meditating. I loved the music she called "Birdies" because of the comforting sounds of nature and birds chirping. Nestling to be close to the music, it filled my ears. It mesmerized me into a deep relaxation as I meditated just like Mom.

After fourteen years with my family, I started getting tired. Then, one day, I knew it was time to leave. I did so with so much comfort as "Birdies" and Mom cradled me into dog heaven. I was a grateful guy. I was loved.

Mason

My new mom told me she liked big male dogs; being a Great Dane, I knew I wouldn't disappoint her. My name, *Mason*, suited my brownish/gray color and potential strength. I grew fast, and smaller dogs could walk under my stance by the time I was eighteen months old, but if I moved too quickly, I'd knock them down. While running, I couldn't always navigate around other dogs, which created an obstacle, so I discovered I could jump over them. It was fun, but maybe that's why they didn't want to play with me. I did my best to be friendly but hoped I wouldn't get an inferiority complex without friends. My mom thinks I'm smart, and her words try to comfort me.

I have many toys, and I know everyone by name. My favorite is a raggedy old stuffed bear, and I'd empty my entire toy box to find *Bear.* As buddies, carrying him in my mouth, sleeping together, and talking to him in whimpers, our friendship has never changed.

Going to daycare a few times a week has helped me with socialization. The people at the daycare give Mom a written report card telling them what I do all day and how I get along with smaller dogs. I'm getting better at accepting my size. An unacceptable report card is when I tear apart other dogs' toys, and Mom must replace them. I wouldn't say I like getting scolded. When I get home, I tell my raggedy old Bear about the trouble I got into. Bear comforts me with his faithful companionship.

When I looked in the mirror and saw how big I was, I understood why other dogs must look up to me. I learned to stretch out on the ground to greet them eye to eye.

Mom found an RV campground and began visiting there often. It had many manicured grassy areas surrounded by thick wood and a fenced-in section where I could sail to my heart's content. One day, a traveling camper's dog growled at me. I looked at him with playful eyes but didn't think he liked me. The dog's owner told me a big burro knocked his mom down. I figured he was protective, so I understood that behavior. No personal offense was taken.

Oh, a happy day! Mom got a job at this RV campground as a greeter and manager. It was like a dream come true. The fenced-in off-leash pet section I often visited was now perfect for me to run and play every day. Dog visitors joined me with playtime, and my daycare socialization skills have paid off. I hope she keeps this job for a long time.

Being unattended in the play area, Mom often checks on me and fills my water dish. It's not that I drink a lot, but I knock the bowl over. I'm clumsy. A fountain in the middle of a pond continually shoots up water. I wish the off-leash park had a rush like that. It's hot in the summer months.

By the end of the day, both Mom and I are exhausted. I play, she works. We like the comfort of the air conditioner when indoors, but insecurity builds up in me. Hearing its roaring and humming sounds makes me defensive. *Is it going to attack me?* I had to find a way to live up to my name, Mason. I'd sneak up to the AC unit and enjoy the tremendous air blowing, but always on guard, just in case of an unexpected confrontation. There has been one challenge after another, but maturing, I'm getting better.

I've learned to play with other dogs and respect their sizes, and my friendliness has taught me to be a big, gentle giant. Mom reassures me of my progress and continues to know my potential. Her smiles and pats on the head display compassion and understanding. She's a great mom!

Maxxine

Happy Birthday! I was a gift to my new Mom on her 50th birthday.

I overheard a conversation about a dog she previously owned and loved named Max. As a loving female replacement, I was given the name Maxxine. Of course, the only thing Max and I had in common was size. German Shepherd dogs are big, so I knew someday I'd be big too. No competition. I was an elegant Standard Poodle.

There was a shopping mall nearby with Mom's favorite store: TJ MAX.[1] Another reason Maxxine became my heartwarming name.

My home was surrounded by three wooded acres with frequent deer visitors. Running with them, I sometimes got lost. After having all that freedom, Mom fenced in an area with new limits. I thought the fence was to keep the flock of wild turkeys away and to guard the house. Maybe it was. Maybe it wasn't. I was still happy.

Being home alone, I wondered where Mom went every day. I found out she was a schoolteacher. Occasionally, there were trips to the playground for a visit. I was

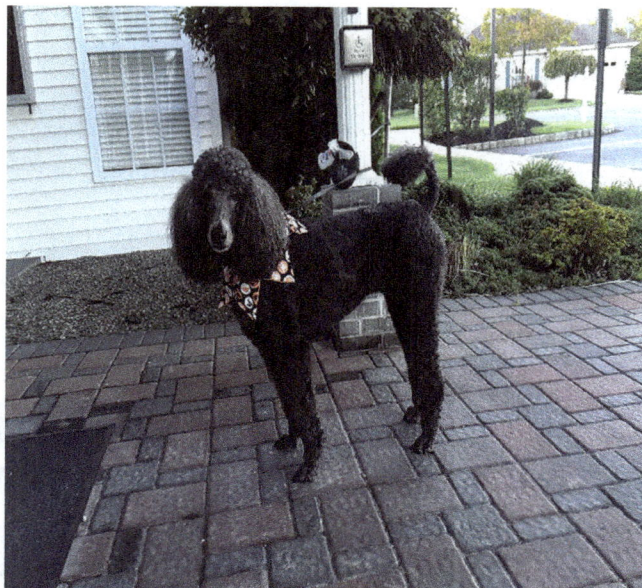

---

[1]   TJ. MAX, a department store chain.

almost as tall as some of the children. Maybe that's why they loved petting me. The attention was great.

Mom found a vest to wear at her favorite store that looked like my curly black hair. She told me the children pretended to pet me whenever she wore it. *Forgotten? Not me; I had a fan club.*

During the summer, there was no school. Hooray! Lots of quality time playing and having regular walks with Mom.

Holidays were for celebration, but one year, on the Fourth of July, I did not celebrate. Mom and I were invited to ride on a pontoon boat. While enjoying the fresh air, a sudden disruption occurred. There was a loud noise of a power washer that startled me.

Without thinking, I jumped out of the boat into the water. By the way, I did have a life jacket on. Unfortunately, my leg got caught in a propeller, and I desperately needed help. In a frantic response, Mom jumped into the water after me. The water that circled me turned red immediately.

My groin was cut open, and everyone panicked on the way to an emergency animal clinic. I survived but was on the disabled list for a long time. An Elizabethan collar was placed around my neck. It was to distract me from my wound. That it did, and weeks later, I forgot what happened. I just wanted out of the collar. Mom was my comforting salvation throughout this horrifying experience. I felt forever indebted to her. After that traumatized event, noises jangled my nerves. Whispers in my ear and a gentle touch from Mom assured me all was well.

Another summer celebration restored my faith when I was invited to a wedding held on Nantucket Island. The reception was under a large tent. There must have been over one hundred people. Parading around like a hostess, I greeted them from person to person. No leash, No restrictions. Freedom! You could be sure I didn't wander near the water.

Mom was a good cook. She grilled sausage, peppers, and onions with homemade New Jersey tomato sauce. A local vegetable garden mart gave her as many tomatoes as needed for this event. I was tall enough to smell and be tempted by all the good stuff on the grill and tables, but Mom was proud of me for not stealing. Rewarded later, I got good food and kept it a secret to keep from tempting others. The guests at the reception had their treats, and I had mine.

"Road trips!" I knew those words. With windows wide open, the breeze flapped and wiggled my ears—another sense of freedom.

Some dogs are resistant to grooming, but not me. I loved the special attention my groomer gave me. We were friends for many years. I confided in her often, and she knew what was on my mind. Loyalty kept our secrets. Getting older slowed me down, and so did the seizures. I didn't want Mom to know about my struggles, but she was intuitive and suspicious.

After 14 years, I locked all those memories in my heart and gave her the key for safekeeping. I'm her hidden treasure. Cuddles and kisses to Mom!

Cookie and Mollie

I was born in Queens, NY. A surprise came to a family when their dog unexpectedly had a litter of Maltipoo puppies. We all needed a home. With ribbons tied around our necks, one by one, each of us was given away as a gift.

My belongings were packed, and I was accepted into a new Long Island, NY home. The name Cookie was befitting to me since I was cute and playful.

Even though Mom had to work, I wasn't a home-alone dog; my Dad was retired. Capturing his affection became my priority. At times, I was confused by my name-calling.

Was it Cookie to come? Or- *Was it Cookie to get a snack?* I answered to both. Being daddy's little girl, I often clung to him. Dad gave me snacks, and I gained weight, and with a fuller belly, Mom made me walk off the calories.

Hustled walks changed my personality, so I began barking a lot. I was following a New York style of communication. No one objected. It was my way of saying *Hello. How are you today?*

One day, I overheard a discussion about getting another dog to live with us. Mom officially was on the lookout for me to have a companion. *What would that mean?*

While grocery shopping, a poster on a community bulletin board caught Mom's attention. There was a picture of a small white dog. It read: **A two-year-old dog needs a home. Housebroken. Does not eat much. Wants a friend.** A military family with a new baby and two young children had transfer orders to another location and wanted to find someone to adopt their dog named *Mollie.*

Mollie was named after the female bulldog mascot of the Marine Corps. But Mollie was far from being a bulldog! She was a Maltipoo, just like Cookie.

My mom responded to the displayed flyer and posed a curious question: "When was Mollie born?" An overwhelming response came from her. "I'll take the dog."

As Mom brought Mollie into our home, she said, "Cookie, I want you to meet your sister, Mollie!" It was true. We both had the same mama. We were twins! *What a surprising coincidence, or was it fate?* Yelping, whimpering, barking, *how was I to react?* Even though I was stunned, I was excited.

My life was never the same again. Mollie and I were inseparable. We slept side by side. I liked a soft bed, but Mollie slept on the floor and preferred a hard surface. I thought sisters thought and acted alike -no such luck.

During our exercise, I walked proudly with my sister, except for when Mollie stopped to eat dried worms she found in the grass. I preferred the soft cookies that Dad gave me. The worms were too crunchy.

Circumstances changed, and Mom had a new job location assignment. We moved to New Jersey. There were many dogs in community-type living, and we befriended one particular male dog named Randy. He often stopped outside our home and waited for us to come and play. *I wondered if Randy liked my sister Mollie more than me since he gave her most of the attention.*

A surprise came on our birthday. It was a cold day in winter, but that didn't deter us from having ice cream as a treat. Mom and Dad sang Elvis Presley's[1] version of Happy Birthday since it was Elvis's birthday, too.

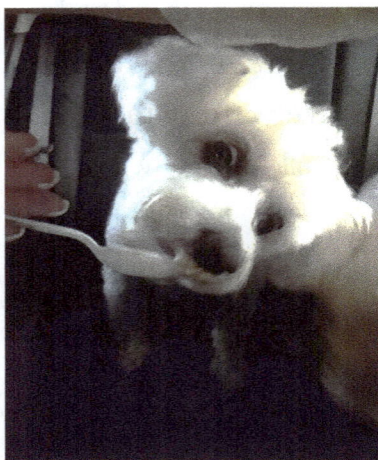

Repeated visits to the ice cream parlor became our ritual. Every time we entered the parking lot, our mouths watered. Whether eating from a spoon or licking a cone, vanilla was our favorite.

Many years have gone by with us as sisters. It was serendipitous how fate brought us back together. Love bonded us forever, and we returned our love to Mom. We all needed each other when our big, cuddly Dad whispered, *"See you on the other side."*

---

[1] Elvis Presley 1935-1977. An American singer and actor.

It was a long walk.
Now we can rest.

Meadow

Being born among the open meadows and tidewater marshes, I received the name *Meadow*. As a puppy, I lived with a gentleman who realized my potential and energy were more than he could handle. I was too young for someone too old.

Luckily, another man came to my rescue. My new home had rolling hills resembling my vast open land, giving me a sense of freedom.

Being a Labrador with an affinity for water, I became his companion. Sporting activities of hunting freshwater fowl included me. *How did I fit in?* At first, I sat in the front of a small boat, wearing an awkward life jacket. I wanted to jump into the water and retrieve a catch, and I followed my instincts. No longer was I a freshwater fishing buddy, but I became a working dog, fetching birds, ducks, and geese.

Soon after that, I graduated to salt water immersion. The ocean had a different movement, and while training to retrieve dummies and sticks, I often got distracted by lifeless seagulls. The scent of seawater on their feathers was a temptation I couldn't resist, and I considered them a delectable treat.

Spinning around in circles for smaller, wiggling sushi became a meal during my ocean trips.

As a companion, those water activities evolved into bonding with this man as my best friend. Tagging along on road trips, shopping, and visiting became official - he was my Dad.

I had a bed in almost every room of the house. Others chuckled, making comments, "It's just a dog." I was more than that; I was a member of the family.

With pride, I started guarding over the acreage that surrounded our residence. The farm had a perfect hill for me to view the land with authority, as I could see far distances with my excellent eyesight. Claiming this mound as my favorite station, I vowed never to leave. It was my domain.

Being a female with a motherly instinct, I was submissive to infants and small children. Allowing them to tug my ears, pull my tongue, and climb on top of me gave them lighthearted pleasure.

When not on duty, I knew how to entertain myself when I was alone, well, almost alone. Grabbing crawling snakes with my mouth, tossing them up in the air, and rolling on them puzzled me as to why these reptiles never fought back. They just played dead. Amusing!

Occasionally, I got into trouble. One day, I ate chocolate eclairs. They didn't taste as good as I anticipated. Pastries were off my list, but chewing on shoes, with their leather taste, was hard to resist. I'll never forget how Dad looked at me with a firm look of discontent. I cowered in the corner but crept slowly towards him afterward and nuzzled my nose beside his leg. All was forgiven.

For sixteen years, my lifeblood was busy hunting, gardening, surveying Dad's land, and being part of his unconditional love. Time took its toll. Struggling to climb in and out of the boat, including going up and down stairs, required effort. Visits to the garden, where I had vegetable snacks, were less frequent. Everything seemed to be exchanged for sleeping more and more. Dad understood my decline.

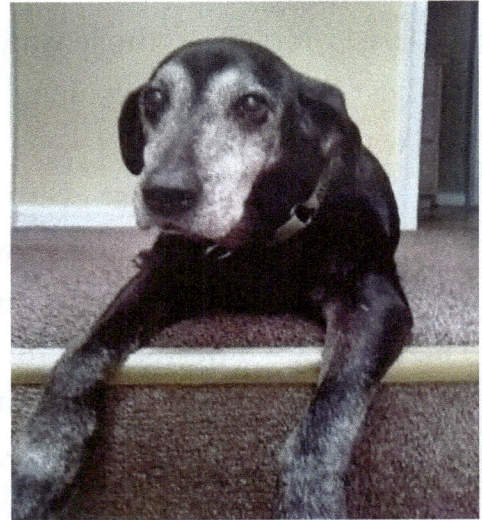

My favorite spot at the top of the hill has cradled me since I was a puppy and beyond. Memories of love never fade away. My Dad's continued emotions are embedded in his mind, "She's not just a dog."

In Memory of Meadow

IN CLOSING

Dear Friends,

Wow! As I sat here in the quietness of this moment and reflected on the undertaking to write this book, I had no idea how much joy would come my way. Getting to know so many amazing dogs and their wonderful owners filled my being with insights into the parallelism of humans and canines. We all reach for the basics of survival, food, shelter, and reproduction. But there is more than that – the emotional side of oneself. It speaks to us without words.

In so many interviews, the stories revealed profoundly touched my heart. Foremost is the unconditional love between owners and their dogs. These animal friends have untiring motivations that cannot be measured as they express whatever experience may come their way. In return, owners forfeit any burden of owning a dog. Why? Their mutual lives together far surpass any hardships. How could one resist the dogs' welcoming and enthusiasm for their owners, no matter the circumstances?

I asked myself, "How could anyone not have a dog?"

Dogs teach us so many things, even though one's thoughts may be that humans train dogs. That's partly true. However, their instincts can also bring out the best in humans. In other words, dogs can train us.

On pondering how many times a day we tell our dog, "I love you," couldn't we take the time to reach out more to our fellowman with the love of kindness, empathy, and forgiveness? It reminds me of a pop hit song recorded in 1965, *What the World Needs Now is Love.*[1] The lyrics talk about love, sweet love, and that we live in a world with too little love. Some readers of this book may remember the song, but others can listen to it on YouTube.com - it's touching.

---

[1] YouTube.com Listen to the 1965 song and lyrics "What the World Needs Now is Love." By Jackie De Shannon

It's enlightening to have written about many rescue dogs. The bottom line message is that everyone who brought those dogs into a forever home and made them part of their family has a heartwarming soul. The shelter workers and the breeders continue to show love for these furry friends, all with the same goal – home, sweet home. Food for Thought: You might open your home to one of these grateful dogs. Aside: OK, if not a dog, get a cat.

I asked myself another question, "What have I learned from each of my special buddies?" - Patience, understanding, compassion, more ways, more ways. STOP. THINK FOR A MOMENT. Ask yourself the same question.

Dogs have given us treasures by remembering how they interacted throughout our lives. My whole world instantly changes around me as I look at my dog sleeping, and in the deep caverns of my mind, I know we are best friends to each other.

Forgive me for being nostalgic. Another pop hit song from 1971, *You Got a Friend*[2] In the lyrics, your friend is always there, whether spring, summer, winter, or fall—another touching song.

In wrapping up these tales, **as told by the dog**, I appreciate every contribution given to me as I wrote about the stars we have in our lives.

In gratitude, I wish you love and peace.

MARY

P.S. And…since there are no conclusions, I ask that you take a few moments to reflect on your gifted treasures.

RANDY

---

[2] YouTube.com . Listen to the 1971 song and lyrics "You Got a Friend," sung and written by Carole King.

ALSO BY DR. MARY B. ANDERSON

Pick-of-the-Day!
Life is like a game, and it's all about
how to Innately play it!

Deck of cards
to accompany the above book

ABOUT THE AUTHOR

Dr. Mary Barnes Anderson has been a dog owner her entire life. Living without a furry friend was never an option. Dogs are unique as she identifies them as companions, comforters, workers, and man's best friend, creating memories never to be forgotten.

While traveling throughout the USA in an RV with her dogs, Anderson had the opportunity to meet numerous adventurous people and their canine buddies. On daily walks through forest trails and parks, she imagined the dogs telling their life stories, which laid the groundwork for this book and motivated her to write. She selected a genre to bring joy into the hearts of the readers.

Anderson retired after thirty-eight years of private practice as a holistic chiropractor. Among her accomplishments are being a professional technique educator, publishing a patient self-help book, and 1989 receiving a prestigious "Doctor of the Year" award from the California Chiropractic Association.

Anderson, over time, included four therapy dogs in her career. Their unconditional acceptance and love for her patients prompted many to exclaim, "Who's the doctor, you or the dog?"

Now residing by the sea on the New Jersey shore with her Lhasa Poo, Randy, her interests remain in science and alternative health. Hobbies include knitting, jigsaw puzzles, board games, and caring for various thriving indoor plants. You can contact this "dog whisperer" at dogstories77@gmail.com

REFERENCES

501(c)(3) organizations. Charities and non-profits are exempt from the IRS. irs.gov/charities-nonprofits

The American Kennel Club (AKC). Founded 1894. A registry of purebred dogs in the USA. The AKC formulated Canine Good Citizen Test Items. akc.org

The Humane Society of the United States. Founded 1953. The nation's most effective animal welfare organization, working to end the suffering of all animals. humanesociety.org

The Soi Dog Foundation. Founded 2003. The mission is to improve the welfare of dogs and cats in Asia, resulting in better lives for both animal and human communities. Headquarters in Thailand. soidog.org

United Blood Trackers Foundation. State legislation varies. Training organizations to track wounded animals by other scents rather than just blood. unitedbloodtrackers.org

A network of over 11,500 rescue shelters for dogs and cats. petfinder.com

YouTube.com is an American online video-sharing and social media platform.

CANINE GOOD CITIZEN TEST ITEMS
Guidelines from the American Kennel Club for Certification

1. **Accepting a friendly stranger.** The evaluator approaches and pretends to shake hands with the handler (hands 6-12" apart). The evaluator does not touch the dog.

2. **Sitting politely for petting.** The evaluator pets the dog; the dog must show no shyness or resentment.

3. **Appearance and grooming.** The evaluator inspects the dog, combs or brushes lightly, and examines ears and each front foot.

4. **Out for a walk.** The handler takes the dog for a short walk, including right turns, left turns, about turns, and stops.

5. **Walking through a crowd.** The dog and the handler walk close to several people; the dog may show casual interest but not jump up.

6. **Sit and down on cue/Staying in place.** The handler shows that the dog can sit and down, then chooses a position, leaves the dog, goes to the end of a 20 ft. line, and returns immediately.

7. **Coming when called.** With the dog still on the 20-ft. line from Test 6, the handler walks out 10 feet and calls the dog.

8. **Reaction to another dog.** Two handlers and dogs approach, pretend to shake hands (hands 6-12" apart), exchange pleasantries, and then move on.

9. **Reaction to distractions.** Distractions are presented; the dog may not panic or show aggression.

10. **Supervised separation.** The handler goes out of sight for 3 minutes. The dog is held on a 6 ft leash by an evaluator.

Search your local American Kennel Club
for evaluators and test areas in your location.

ACKNOWLEDGEMENTS

Being thankful is a primary requisite for a contented life.

Thank you to the many people I met while RVing and their loyal furry friends. Even though I may never see or meet some of them again, they were the ones who sparked the idea to write this book.

A special thank you to those who shared their enthusiasm for relaying stories of their best canine companions, many of whom I have met at Freedom Fields County Park in Little Egg Harbor, NJ.

An appreciation to all those who joyfully gave me photos of their dogs.

Thank you to the Manahawkin NJ Writers' Group for their support as each story was presented.

I sincerely appreciate Linda Pepe for the time she spent reviewing my writings during my entire process. Her gracious mannerism has been a gift.

A special thank you to my son Dennis for titling this book.

Gratitude and love to all those who have encouraged me, especially Rick Muir, Jayne Dickenson, my son Richard, and my daughter-in-law, Colleen.

All this was completed with the help of Randy, my sweetheart dog.

From all of us,
THANK YOU
for volunteering and donating to
animal shelters and rescue centers.